The Green Pastures

Wisconsin/Warner Bros. Screenplay Series

Editorial Board

Dudley Andrew
Tino Balio, *General Editor*
John G. Cawelti
Dore Schary

The Green Pastures

Edited with an introduction by

Thomas Cripps

Published for the Wisconsin Center for Film and Theater Research by
The University of Wisconsin Press

Published 1979

The University of Wisconsin Press
114 North Murray Street
Madison, Wisconsin 53715

The University of Wisconsin Press, Ltd.
1 Gower Street
London WC1E 6HA, England

First printing

Printed in the United States of America

For LC CIP information see the colophon

ISBN 0-299-07920-1 cloth; 0-299-07924-4 paper

Publication of this volume has been assisted by a grant from
The Brittingham Fund, Inc.

Contents

Foreword

In donating the Warner Film Library to the Wisconsin Center for Film and Theater Research in 1969, along with the RKO and Monogram film libraries and UA corporate records, United Artists created a truly great resource for the study of American film. Acquired by United Artists in 1957, during a period when the major studios sold off their films for use on television, the Warner library is by far the richest portion of the gift, containing eight hundred sound features, fifteen hundred short subjects, nineteen thousand still negatives, legal files, and press books, in addition to screenplays for the bulk of the Warner Brothers product from 1930 to 1950. For the purposes of this project, the company has granted the Center whatever publication rights it holds to the Warner films. In so doing, UA has provided the Center another opportunity to advance the cause of film scholarship.

Our goal in publishing these Warner Brothers screenplays is to explicate the art of screenwriting during the thirties and forties, the so-called Golden Age of Hollywood. In preparing a critical introduction and annotating the screenplay, the editor of each volume is asked to cover such topics as the development of the screenplay from its source to the final shooting script, differences between the final shooting script and the release print, production information, exploitation and critical reception of the film, its historical importance, its directorial style, and its position within the genre. He is also encouraged to go beyond these guidelines to incorporate supplemental information concerning the studio system of motion picture production.

We could set such an ambitious goal because of the richness of the script files in the Warner Film Library. For many film titles, the files might contain the property (novel, play, short story, or original story idea), research materials, variant drafts of scripts

7

(from story outline to treatment to shooting script), post-production items such as press books and dialogue continuities, and legal records (details of the acquisition of the property, copyright registration, and contracts with actors and directors). Editors of the Wisconsin/Warner Bros. Screenplay Series receive copies of all the materials, along with prints of the films (the most authoritative ones available for reference purposes), to use in preparing the introductions and annotating the final shooting scripts.

In the process of preparing the screenplays for publication, typographical errors were corrected, punctuation and capitalization were modernized, and the format was redesigned to facilitate readability. The illustrations are frame enlargements taken from a 35-mm print of the film provided by United Artists.

In theory, the Center should have received the extant scripts of all pre-1951 Warner Brothers productions when the United Artists Collection was established. Recent events, however, have created at least some doubt in this area. Late in 1977, Warners donated collections consisting of the company's production records and distribution records to the University of Southern California and Princeton University respectively. The precise contents of the collections are not known, since at the present time they are not generally open to scholars. To the best of our knowledge, all extant scripts have been considered in the preparation of these volumes. Should any other versons be discovered at a later date, we will recognize them in future printings of any volumes so affected.

Tino Balio
General Editor

Acknowledgments

I am grateful for the opportunity the Wisconsin Center for Film and Theater Research offered me to attempt a published edition of *The Green Pastures*. Marc Connelly generously gave me an afternoon's interview that provided insights that could have come from no other source. At a crucial moment, Miles Krueger, director of the Institute of the American Musical, provided important information. David Berger of Towson State University kindly gave me access to equipment that allowed me to view the film systematically. Professor Walter Fisher and then-Dean Richard I. McKinney of Morgan State University read parts of the manuscript and discussed theological history. William Forshaw of the Enoch Pratt Free Library provided the basis for a better understanding of Roark Bradford's work in several conversations.

Over many years of work on other projects, my knowledge of *The Green Pastures* grew through the efforts of the librarians of the institutions cited in the footnotes. They include the Wisconsin Center for Film and Theater Research, the Schomburg Collection of the New York Public Library, the Library of Performing Arts of the New York Public Library, the Humanities Division of the Enoch Pratt Free Library, the Oral History Collection of Columbia University, the James Weldon Johnson Collection of Beineke Library of Yale University, the Manuscript Division and the Motion Picture and Television Division of the Library of Congress, and the Soper Library of Morgan State University.

I am in the debt of these friends and strangers who should not, however, be held accountable for what resulted from their kindness.

My children have grown up bearing the burden of a father who has spent more time in libraries than he has with them. To them—

Acknowledgments

Paul, Alma, and Ben—I dedicate my part of this book as a small measure of my pride in their survival powers (and of my appreciation for their mother's fortitude).

T.C.

Introduction
A Monument to Lost Innocence

Thomas Cripps

In order to appreciate the achievement of Marc Connelly's *The Green Pastures*, the play and the motion picture must be seen as two points along the continuum of American social and political life. The film is important to us not only as a monument to a lost past and as a prophecy but also as a cinematic accomplishment; similarly, the play is important as both a social document and a theatrical moment.

Like many other Pulitzer Prize winners, the play carried a message that spoke more to its own times than to the ages. By 1930, the year Connelly's "fable" began its long run, urban Afro-America had begun to achieve a self-conscious social identity that had often been denied in the rural South, and with this newly citified black life had come a certain fame for "the new Negro." For white Americans, the increasingly visible evidence of the breadth and variety of black culture began to give the lie to generations of invidious stereotypes that had caricatured Negroes in advertising, performing arts, popular fiction, doggerel, and jokes. Coincident with the migration of southern blacks to north-ern cities, Hollywood movies began to redirect their depictions of blacks on the screen away from abject slaveys and toadies toward sentimental tributes to such presumed "good Negro" virtues as loyalty and fortitude in the face of hard times. Six months before *The Green Pastures* appeared on Broadway, two black Hollywood films reflected the new sensibility: MGM's *Hallelujah!* and Fox's *Hearts in Dixie*. These interacting forces of black urbanization and white attention to it together provided an intellectual and social environment in which Connelly wrote *The Green Pastures* and directed the movie five years later.

In times of social upheaval, romance has often been the vehicle for conveying a sense of lost innocence. Wordsworth's pastoral lyrics, Scott's Gothic novels, and Constable's great green landscapes spoke to the sense of loss and provided respite from the wrenching forces of the British industrial revolution. So too, Connelly's fable of black folk religion appeared at the end of the first decade in which blacks and whites self-consciously confronted each other across the boundaries of their urban neighborhoods. The sense of lost innocence and of disappearing rural, primitive folklore that would soon be no more informed and colored Connelly's scenes.

The Green Pastures came to Broadway just as economic depression began to dampen optimism, impoverish the cities blacks had begun to fill, and dry up the sources of wealth that had fueled the "Harlem Renaissance." Connelly's fable romanticized and memorialized the history of the rural black South that had been decimated by the northern black diaspora and, in disarming style, brought it to a broad national white audience for whom black life had been exotic.

Connelly's dramatic strategy was a simple one. Taking as his source Roark Bradford's local-color genre stories of black southern life, *Ol' Man Adam an' His Chillun*, he created a company of black characters who wrestled with the universal problem of man's nature and his place in the cosmos. Gone were the black brutes, mindless Topsies, and blindly loyal uncles of southern legend. Taking a critical moment in Old Testament theology, the metamorphosis of Jehovah from a wrathful tribal God into the merciful God promised by the prophet Hosea, Connelly recast the myth into terms that a southern black preacher might have used to explain Genesis to his Sunday school pupils. From Connelly's pristine heaven, God descends to earth in four crucial episodes of Judeo-Christian legend: the creation and fall from grace, the deluge, the Hebrew exodus from Egypt and captivity in Babylon, and an apocryphal tale that foreshadows the crucifixion. The resulting structure allowed audiences to see man's growth toward a modern spirit as part of a black myth that conveniently held

white America blameless for the plight of blacks, because as sur-
rogates for all of mankind the black characters struggled, not
against external enemies, but against their own nature expressed
as inner weakness to be overcome through prayer and faith. Thus
the black company of more than one hundred characters became
a collective symbol of man's hope and spirit. Connelly's movie,
then, is to be studied not only as cinema but as a document of
American social history and as a well-meaning attempt to present
the best of the black soul in a pleasing way to an urbane white
audience.

The drama from which the film emerged arrived at the end of
an era during which white New Yorkers, long before the rest of
their countrymen, had seen urban, prepossessing black Americans who were far removed from the southern rural blacks of
American legend. In the 1920s, major white publishers had brought
black novelists and poets to the attention of a white readership,
preparing the way for a modification of American race relations.
The trend took two forms, one intellectual, the other popular. The
former used the art of Countee Cullen, Claude McKay, Rudolph
Fisher, and Jean Toomer to bring home the social reality of black
life; the latter won the affection of a broad popular white audience through the vaudeville and film work of Bert Williams and
later Stepin Fetchit and Bill Robinson.

This is not to say that America's racial attitudes and customs
were transformed by a few black poets sipping tea in bohemian
salons or by a couple of hoofers clicking their ways across vaudeville stages. Nevertheless, independently of each other, and often
burdened with mutual cross-purposes and antipathies, through
their arts and through intellectual inquiry or the mere winning of
affection across racial lines, black writers and performers contrib-
uted to the withering away of outmoded nineteenth-century racial
behaviors. To expect more is to ignore the stamina of segregation
customs.

Negro Theater in the Twenties

Connelly's play provided a neat punctuation to the end of the era
of the Harlem Renaissance by paying homage to black folk reli-

gion while taming white anxieties aroused by the northward migration of southern Negroes. The 1920s had begun with a blossoming of Negro theater and ended with a romantic white version of it for a large and appreciative white audience. By speaking to this mood, Connelly clearly earned his Pulitzer.

James Weldon Johnson, the executive secretary of the National Association for the Advancement of Colored People and a shewd observer of black theater, reckoned the beginning of the era at the appearance of Ridgely Torrence's *Three Plays for a Negro Theatre* on April 5, 1917, one day before America entered World War I. For Johnson it was the Negro's "first opportunity in serious legitimate drama." He wrote in the *New York Age:* "We do not know how many colored people of greater New York realize that April, 1917, marks an epoch for the Negro on stage."[1] Torrence, a white man, was soon joined in the trend by other whites: Eugene O'Neill with *The Emperor Jones* (with Charles Gilpin in the title role) and *All God's Chillun Got Wings* at the Provincetown Playhouse; Paul Green with his Pulitzer-winning play, *In Abraham's Bosom;* and young Charles MacArthur and Edward Sheldon (author of the notorious *The Nigger*) with the flashy Harlem melodrama *Lulu Belle.*[2]

Away from white Broadway, black theater also bloomed. University theaters, such as Howard's Ira Aldridge Players, were joined by the Pekin stock company in Chicago, Karamu House in Cleveland, and the Lafayette Players in Harlem. They intruded into white circles in two ways: white visitors came to black preserves, especially Harlem, and black productions, such as *Shuffle Along,* played Broadway during the off months. Negro revues that lent themselves to formulaic repetition perpetuated the trend. Two performers in the cast of *Shuffle Along,* for example, soon wrote

1. Edith J. R. Isaacs, *The Negro in the American Theatre* (New York: McGrath, 1947), p. 59.

2. Isaacs, *Negro in American Theatre*, p. 82. *Lulu Belle* was an ambiguity. On the one hand, Isaacs claimed that it "hastened the presentation of other plays of Negro life especially those with Harlem as a background," but on the other, the producer, David Belasco, hedged by casting it with the white actors Lenore Ulric and Henry Hull.

their own *Chocolate Dandies,* which was in turn followed by annual productions of Lew Leslie's *Blackbirds* and lesser known musical rambles.[3]

The rage for black performing arts coincided with the maturing of American theater from its nineteenth-century days of melodrama and flamboyant actor-managers. After World War I, the Playwrights' Company, the American National Theatre, the Theatre Guild, and the Group Theatre helped bring substantive social themes to the boards. Thus Connelly's *The Green Pastures* arrived on Broadway after audiences had received ten years of tutelage in social drama. Indeed, Connelly may have been inspired as much by DuBose and Dorothy Heyward's *Porgy,* a 1926 Theatre Guild production directed by Rouben Mamoulian that owed its own inspiration to the black folk life of the Sea Islands of South Carolina, as by Roark Bradford's book.[4] Eight years later, *Porgy* may have attracted Warner Brothers to Connelly's script when the Heywards' play reappeared as an opera, possibly assuring the studio of the continuing popularity of Negro themes.

Movies followed the trend. In 1928, King Vidor, after months of pleading, persuaded MGM to produce *Hallelujah!*, fulfilling his longtime urge to film rural Negro life. At Fox, Paul J. Sloane expanded a short subject into still another fragile rendering of Negro folk life, the studio's "prestige" film of the year, *Hearts in Dixie.* While the other studios avoided such risky themes, they

3. Isaacs, *Negro in American Theatre,* pp. 61, 63, 66. At least one black historian looked with indifference upon the opening of Broadway to black talent. In the view of Loften Mitchell, the trend was merely a restoration of the Negro to the stage from which he had been segregated as a consequence of the 1896 monopoly of Broadway by the Theatrical Trust Syndicate. Blacks were driven to indigenous theater such as the Krigwa Players and the Negro Art Theatre. See Loften Mitchell, *Black Drama: The Story of the American Negro in the Theatre* (New York: Hawthorn, 1967), chapter 7, and John Selby, *Beyond Civil Rights* (Cleveland: World, 1966).

4. Mitchell, *Black Drama,* pp. 83–86. It must be remembered that romance has its uses. Seen through the mists of time and place, *The Green Pastures,* in the words of the critic, Kenneth Burke, carried audiences "into a region of gentleness, this in contrast with the harsh demand of our day." Quoted in Doris E. Abramson, *Negro Playwrights in the American Theatre, 1925–1959* (New York: Columbia University Press, 1969), p. 53.

made a long cycle of two-reelers featuring black music if not black life.[5]

Connelly and the Play

Like many middle-class Americans, Connelly maintained an affectionate neutrality toward Afro-Americans, sympathizing with their plight, enjoying the company of the few blacks who served them, and condemning the worst of "southern outrages." Like another Pittsburgher, Stephen Foster, he perceived Negro life as a romance for which his own life had done little to prepare him. Of his only early contact with a black he recalled: "We had a Negro porter called Jim with whom I had the intimacy of a nine-year-old boy. He had an almost slavelike care and concern for me. . . . That's my only experience with Negroes."[6]

His childhood in McKeesport and Pittsburgh, in comfortable circumstances, was filled with gentle good times leavened by talks with actors, like Richard Mansfield, who stayed at his father's hotel. Until the "rich man's panic" of 1907, nothing, not even the death of his father in 1902, disturbed the tranquility. Then in 1908, his mother lost the hotel and opened a small shop in Pittsburgh, and Connelly, instead of going to Harvard, joined in turn the *Pittsburgh Press* as a collector of advertising fees, the Associated Press as a rewrite man, and the *Pittsburgh Gazette-Times* as a humor columnist in the style of Franklin P. Adams. Along the way he tinkered with skits, plays, songs, and stories that led him to Broadway where, as World War I ended, he began a collaboration with another Pittsburgher, George S. Kaufman, the *Times* drama critic. *Dulcy*, their first script (a light comedy intended as a vehicle for young Lynn Fontanne), began Connelly's celebrated career, which was punctuated by evenings at the opera, drinks at W. C. Fields's private bar, and long lunches with a circle of young

5. Thomas Cripps, *Slow Fade to Black: The Negro in American Film, 1900–1942* (New York: Oxford University Press, 1977), chapter 10.

6. Interview with Marc Connelly, New York, April 15, 1978. Like many northern liberals of his day, Connelly associated racism with southern provincialism, which he held in obvious contempt.

writers at the Algonquin Hotel and the studio of the magazine illustrator Neysa McMein.[7]

A life so successful as to resemble a bad play seemed to leave no room for attention to black life, at least until a warm day, probably in 1928, when his friend Rollin Kirby, the Pulitzer-winning cartoonist, pressed upon him a copy of *Ol' Man Adam an' His Chillun*, which he read in a single night's sitting.[8] Late in the year, Connelly signed a contract with Harper and Brothers publishers assigning him the right to make a play from Bradford's book, in return for which Bradford was to receive a generous thirty percent of the royalties and a quarter of the sale of motion picture rights.[9]

Bradford's book accelerated the calm rhythm of Connelly's stroll toward success. Trained by a decade of theatrical collaboration that coincided with a pervasive boom in racial productions on Broadway, Connelly took up the challenge of bringing *Ol' Man Adam an' His Chillun* to the stage as *The Green Pastures*. Unschooled in black lore, he set sail on the steamer *Dixie* to see Louisiana, hear the local dialect, and learn the lore at the feet of Bradford.

Like other southern white writers of his day, Bradford viewed black life from the verandah of the big house, a fact reflected in the illustrations of the first edition, which depicted God not as black but "as a stereotype southern planter with black fedora hat, goatee, and cane." Yet, if Connelly cleaved to Bradford's conception of pious, long-suffering Negro folk, he also wisely saw that God must emerge as a strong black figure. In addition, he provided his own apocrypha in which he sketched an archetype of

---

7. Marc Connelly, *Voices Offstage: A Book of Memoirs* (New York: Holt, Rinehart & Winston, 1968), chapter 4.

8. Connelly's recollection of this incident varies. See Connelly, *Voices Offstage*, p. 144; Oral History Collection, Columbia University, Popular Arts Series II, p. 527; Connelly interview; Paul T. Nolan, *Marc Connelly* (New York: Twayne Publishers, 1969), pp. 79–80. See Roark Bradford, *Ol' Man Adam an' His Chillun: Being the Tales They Tell About the Time When the Lord Walked the Earth Like a Natural Man*, with drawings by A. B. Walker (New York: Harper, 1928).

9. Letter from Eugene F. Saxton to Connelly, September 28, 1928.

the new Negro who spoke to the question of a militant black future in urban America: his Hezdrel defends Jerusalem against a nameless enemy.

It is Hezdrel who marks the thematic difference between *Ol' Man Adam an' His Chillun* and *The Green Pastures*, as shown most vividly in the denouement of the two pieces. Through Hezdrel, Connelly was able to close on a note of affirmation that, while it lacked specific political conviction or affiliation, clearly promised, to black audiences at least, a future in which they could become activists in their own cause. In this sense, any reasonably "good race man" could view *The Green Pastures* as an allegory in which his own activism was in a great tradition of fighters for Hebrew and Negro freedom from bondage. Connelly brought this special relationship between the Jewish and Negro heritages into the present by ending with the fulfillment of the biblical prophecy of a messiah. This beginning of the salvationist ethic of the New Testament and its merciful God to whom blacks may pray for redemption occurs in the last moment off stage in the drama and out of frame in the film. Thus the great history of Jews is inherited by modern blacks.

Bradford's book of stories, on the other hand, promises only business as usual as far as blacks are concerned. Joshua's assault on Jericho is merely one of a series of God's stunts rather than an embryonic political expression, as in the film. Bradford's younger generation is represented not by militant Hezdrel but by Ehud, whose courage is displayed not in combat but in a street-style stabbing. And his promise of the future is that nothing will change. His Nigger Deemus, for example, knows God represents the status quo. "Lawd, you knows and I knows I ain't got no business goin' round de wilderness wid you and all dem white folks," he says. "I knows my place in dis man's town." Only in heaven does he expect a reward that includes the knowledge that "won't nobody know is I white or black." In fact, God is as devious as other white men in racial matters. While pleading that "I ain't got no Jim Crow law 'mongst my disciples," he treats Nigger Deemus to a display of racial discrimination that reminds the Negro of the white-primary election laws and "grandfather clauses" used to deny blacks the franchise in the South. Miraculously, God trans-

forms rocks into food for his disciples, while denying food to
Nigger Deemus on various disingenuous pretexts. At last, after
each disciple has received his fried chicken, ham, cake, and beans,
old Nigger Deemus is left with "a little bitty hard lump er cold
cawn bread."

It may be seen from Bradford's reportage of southern life as it
was that Connelly performed a considerable feat of creative imagination by taking his inspiration from a work in which whites had
their accustomed place at the top and reworking it into a fable
possessed of a warm black soul. Perhaps Hezdrel was Connelly's
northern sensibility grafted onto Bradford's deep South.

He finished the first act on board the *Dixie* and, after a day's
warm acquaintance with Bradford, began to select the music, with
the help of Negro musicians near Bradford's home in the Vieux
Carré. A few visits to black churches and the Mississippi Valley to
the north, and Connelly began to shape the stylized dramaturgy
of *The Green Pastures*.[10]

Connelly's Yankee sensibility, somewhat like the intense but
surface view of the tourist, both helped and hindered his work.
His sympathetic liberalism brought dignity to his black characters. But he missed much. Myriad historical, social, and doctrinal
reasons for the splintering of Negro churches were reduced to
petty quarrels over social dancing. He met not a spectrum of
preachers but "a dozen Mr. Deshees" on his rural jaunts. For his
notion of sin he turned to a few " 'barrelhouse' dives" in New
Orleans and, "in a way, possibly," his recollections of Harlem
hustlers and criminals. Out in the countryside, he read dialogue
to the field hands for their approval, much as he imagined "Robert Burns's habit of reading his poems in dialect to the peasants
for criticisms of their authenticity." After a year that included
tinkering with the script on a cruise through the Greek islands,
he completed an acceptable draft and began making the rounds
of producers.[11]

10. Connelly, *Voices Offstage*, p. 148; Connelly interview. Connelly chose the
steamer rather than the train in order to allow him time to concentrate on writing.

11. Connelly, *Voices Offstage*, pp. 150, 153, 164. In interview, Connelly provided
an addendum to his recollection of "sin" in New Orleans. He cited his visits to

Not only had the Great Crash decimated the ranks of prospective producers, but veterans of "the street" greeted *The Green Pastures* with skepticism because of the "bad business" promised by its black and possibly sacrilegious theme. Successful black shows had always laid claim to jazzy music and scandalous characters, or, like *Shuffle Along*, they had survived a tryout in some disused theater. Besides, there was no hope for an eventual sale to Hollywood; *Hearts in Dixie* and *Hallelujah!* had not stimulated a trend.[12]

Nevertheless, Rowland Stebbins, a retired stockbroker with an itch for show business, became an "angel." His bridge partner, George S. Kaufman, had touted the script and caught Stebbins's interest, and by December 29 rehearsals began for an opening on February 26, 1930.

Of all the problems, including working in the shabby halls available to Negro companies, casting was the most difficult. They were agreed that native dignity should matter as much as acting experience and therefore searched outside the thin ranks of Negro thespians. Connelly reached into the South, inquiring after the availability of Robert Russa Moton, the principal of world-famous Tuskegee Institute, to play God. Failing that, and with only four days left before the opening of rehearsals, they just missed signing Adam Clayton Powell, Sr., of Harlem's Abyssinian Baptist Church, for the role of God. At the last moment, they auditioned Richard B. Harrison, a touring platform speaker and dramatic reader and a perfect typecast as a patriarchal God, who agreed to play the role only after assurances that the play would in no way slander the race.[13]

The Green Pastures immediately began its career as an American classic, an event that memorialized, celebrated, romanticized, and embalmed lost values while offering them as the foundation of the present. It presented Afro-Americans as interracial ambassadors of goodwill whose charming flaws of dialect and naiveté al-

Harlem "when there was something to see" as at least a possible additional source for his depiction of evil.

12. Columbia Oral History Collection, p. 527; Connelly, *Voices Offstage*, p. 165.

13. Columbia Oral History Collection, pp. 527–28; Connelly, *Voices Offstage*, pp. 167–79, 171–72, 175, 190.

lowed white audiences to admire their unthreatening dignity under duress. For blacks, at least those who praised it, the play fulfilled an ambition that most black leaders, even the most nationalistic, had come to embrace—the eventual carving of a black place in American society based upon individual dignity and merit. It was as though Marc Connelly spoke for the achievement-oriented black middle class.

The Green Pastures, like Stepin Fetchit's movie roles, became a tactic in a kind of advertising campaign designed to evoke interracial affection. As Fetchit often described his act as a device for relieving white unease in dealing with racial matters, so Connelly felt that his play and Harrison's performance stimulated "the audience's affectionate responses."[14] A typical friendly reviewer accounted for the success of the play with reference to its ambassadorial intent: "All the way through it is permeated by affection for and understanding of the half-developed negro yearning" for biblical truth.[15] James Weldon Johnson agreed that affection was at the center of both Fetchit and *The Green Pastures*—with a caveat that neither should be taken as the reality of Negro life.

Generally, white critics praised Connelly's attempt at affectionate universality, his sincerity, and his lack of patronizing—sometimes by patronizing *him*. As Richard Watts wrote in the *New York Post* (March 22, 1930): "Perhaps the most amazing thing about the play is that its author should be a white man, a sophisticated New Yorker, hitherto distinguished chiefly as a wit and a satirist."

Watts was also the only urban critic who demurred from the praise of *The Green Pastures*, having been discomfited by his misunderstanding of Connelly's apocryphal Hezdrel who symbolized a modern teleology in which the new Negro took up arms against his oppressors. He found Hezdrel's scene the "one place in the narrative where the author appears to lose, for a moment, his objective view-point; where you begin to suspect that he is stepping out of character and showing you something, not as it

14. Connelly, *Voices Offstage*, p. 187.
15. *Tatler* (London), June 25, 1930, Carl Van Vechten Collection, Yale University.

appears to an old Negro preacher, but as the more sophisticated playwright has fabricated it." For him Hezdrel conveyed the message of the play "that is not quite in the mood of strict simplicity that the rest of the play maintains." In other words, where an aggressive Negro appears, Watts blamed Connelly's loss of balance, perhaps because Hezdrel's assault on a nameless enemy broke the spell of the audience's warm feelings toward Negroes.

The black press leapt at the opportunity to praise a white liberal theatrical production that accomplished the black goal of dampening white antipathy. Few of them ventured to attack that which whites had praised; they too romanticized slavery into an epoch that tempered the survival powers of the race. Others routinely praised any black achievement, whatever its merits, especially if white intellectuals had put their imprimatur upon it or white entrepreneurs had bought advertising lineage for it.

Through the medium of show business, the black press also discovered a way of mythologizing black performers into icons that symbolized the two goals of individual success and racial integration, without sacrificing claims to Negro cultural nationalism. The *Pittsburgh Courier* (February 22, 1930), a pioneer in its coverage of theater, for example, praised Jules Bledsoe's work in *Show Boat* as "ample proof that real ability knows no color barrier" while admiring the chorus line for its "haunting rhythm and melody which is a heritage of the Negro." Expressed as formula, blacks were entitled to the same opportunities accorded other Americans while retaining preternatural traits to which whites were not privy.

Turning to *The Green Pastures*, the *Courier*'s Chappie Gardner paid tribute to both elements of the myth, white homage and black attainment. He gave credit to Connelly for rendering black religion "in a lovable and simple way" unspoiled by "irreverence" while accurately recreating "a fishfry in heaven much the same as we [blacks] give picnics today. . . . Everyone," he reckoned, "should see this play."[16]

With variations, other black papers agreed. New York's *Amster-*

16. That Connelly's play inadvertently gave him a reputation as a racial ambassador may be seen in later events. During World War II, when the Army was beset by racial violence surrounding and even on its reservations, the Pentagon asked

dam News headlined its story: "Green Pastures Takes Broadway by Storm." Claude A. Barnett's Associated Negro Press, which reached a nationwide sample of black papers, celebrated the event as the occasion on which black and white liberals could agree. One such story that appeared in the *Norfolk Journal and Guide* (March 8, 1930) quoted a platoon of white New York critics whose praise was ratified by Walter White of the NAACP, who pointed out that Connelly's "moving pageant" illustrated the affinity between the plight of ancient Jews and modern Negroes.

Even if black critics demurred from the praise of *The Green Pastures*, they agreed that the race benefited from the employment it brought black actors. Bennie Butler in the gossipy *Inter-State Tatler* (March 14, 1930), for example, predicted that "this triumph will eventually mean to the colored entertainers . . . [a] harvest" of jobs derived from road companies and imitators. "While things look bad for the rest of the country," he wrote, "the sepia theatre entertainers can look forward to an era of prosperity."

As the bearers of the theatrical fable, the actors became a focal point of discussion that threatened to spoil the journalistic unanimity. When Connelly, intending a bit of well-meaning praise, claimed that "almost every Negro is a good actor," the *Journal and Guide* (March 15, 1930) challenged the "press agents and white producers . . . pernicious habit of depriving Negro talent of any recognition of its past achievements" by asserting that blacks were no more than "uncultivated talent found in kitchens and divers other menial jobs." The *Courier* (May 24, 1930) carried the argument to the actors themselves, asking them, in view of their public roles, to abstain from the gambling, tardiness, and scandals that always threatened the survival of plays like *The Green Pastures*. "It is always the same with colored casts," said the *Courier*'s critic. "They cry for opportunities, but when they are fortunate enough to get hold of one, they deliberately throw it away."

Connelly to study the problem and to submit suggestions that eventually grew into the training film *The Negro Soldier*. And when Walter White of the NAACP opened a wartime campaign to compel Hollywood to broaden the range of black roles, MGM hired Connelly to do a draft of *Cabin in the Sky*. White also proposed that Connelly write a film biography of black agronomist George Washington Carver (Correspondence in NAACP Records, Library of Congress).

As the most influential black voices of organized, affiliated, middle-class Negroes, the house organs of the NAACP and the Urban League reached the broadest audience of black intellectuals and spoke with the clearest authority. The Urban League not only used the drama as the occasion for a benefit performance, but its magazine, *Opportunity*, praised it as an uplifting experience that "transcends the color line."[17] *Crisis*, the NAACP organ, hedged because of "the embargo which white wealth lays on full Negro expression," but concluded that *The Green Pastures* was "beautiful and beautifully done, . . . the beginning of a new era, not simply in Negro art but in the art of America."[18]

Even after a half year's reflection, few black intellectuals damned the play. The *Chicago Defender*, Theophilus Lewis, and George S. Schuyler took sharpest issue with the majority. Lewis found it a merely "fair to middling play" saved by "astute direction," while Schuyler refused to see it at all because of the old-fashioned stereotyping that had been reported to him. One of the actors, Salem Tutt Whitney, reminded black critics of the old Negro custom of refraining from intraracial criticism within earshot of whites. "There are some things that a critic should not write even if he thinks them," wrote Whitney, but Schuyler waived the rejoinder aside as a self-serving defense of his "meal ticket."[19]

Connelly himself had taken pains to avoid such division even before the play opened. Against the advice of his producer, he cut the parable of David and Goliath during rehearsals. If the Egyptian captivity of the Hebrews symbolized slavery in Negro minds, then David's clash with the champion of the Philistines could only stand for oppressive whites bent on reenslaving blacks. On the eve of the fight, Samuel wails, "An' now de Chosen People is abandoned." Can he mean, unconsciously, that Republicans had abandoned the Negro during Reconstruction at the end of their American captivity? God answers by helping David. Are we to

17. Howard Bradstreet, "A Negro Miracle Play," *Opportunity*, May 1930, pp. 150–51.
18. *Crisis*, May 1930, pp. 162, 177.
19. *Amsterdam News* (New York), March 5 and October 8, 1930.

24

believe that God helps blacks make war on whites? If so, then the principle of universality is an empty one.[20]

The Green Pastures embarked upon a five-year career on Broadway and the road, with the blessing of black and white critics. As a fable that symbolized the American accommodation to a racial history that granted black suffering without requiring whites to feel guilt, the drama became a powerful document in the history of popular art. Unfortunately for its prospects as a movie, by the time it lumbered into production in 1935, American racial sensibility had begun to change under the liberal, if inconsistent, prodding of New Deal rhetoric. The movie could make only a fraction of the monumental impact of the Broadway production; it neither celebrated nor memorialized racial history; it merely repeated itself.

Production of the Film

By 1935, the year Connelly signed his contract with Warner Brothers for a $100,000 advance against the profits, too much had changed. Only two months before the pact, Rose McClendon, the doyenne of Negro theater, had written an angry letter not to the black *Amsterdam News* but to the white *New York Times* (June 6, 1935), announcing that the day was past when blacks contented themselves with a mere presence on the stage. Instead, they demanded that theater "deal with Negroes, with Negro problems, with phases of Negro life, faithfully presented and accurately delineated." As evidence she contrasted a "doomed" black version of *The Front Page* at Harlem's Lafayette with Clifford Odets's agitprop *Waiting for Lefty*, which attracted four thousand to the Negro People's Theatre.

American films had also slipped to the left between 1930 and 1935. At first, blacks appeared in largely ceremonial roles depicting their fortitude in the face of southern racism or as natural men possessed of wisdom inaccessible to effete white men. *Hearts in Dixie, Hallelujah!*, Universal's *Uncle Tom's Cabin* (1927), a revival of

20. In an interview, Connelly found the scene merely "gratuitous." It may be found in Connelly, *Voices Offstage*, pp. 178–83.

The Birth of a Nation with a sound track, and even films inspired by blackface minstrelsy spoke for the era. But after 1935, black roles broadened to include the outraged black family of Odets's *Golden Boy*, the smooth gunman of *The Petrified Forest*, and musical numbers inspired by Etta Moten's singing of "Remember My Forgotten Man" in *Gold Diggers of 1933*. Some of them conveyed mild propaganda messages such as the antilynching tracts, Mervyn LeRoy's *They Won't Forget*, and Fritz Lang's *Fury*. Others, like *Show Boat*, were merely strengthened by fresh performers, like Paul Robeson, who offered alternatives to the work of such Hollywood regulars as Bill Robinson, who supported Shirley Temple in *The Little Colonel* and *The Littlest Rebel*.[21] In *Slave Ship, So Red the Rose*, and *The Prisoner of Shark Island*, slavery received less than its often rose-tinted treatment. Moreover, Negroes often took note of the events. As the white literateur Carl Van Vechten wrote to his black friend James Weldon Johnson: "Have you seen 'Slave Ship'? This goes a little further in the direction of realism than most movies on this subject and you get a glimpse of how the Africans were packed into the holds of ships and treated."[22]

Sometimes the pace of change seemed too rapid. The usually liberal *Variety* complained of an interracial routine played by Martha Raye and Louis Armstrong in *Artists and Models*: "This inter-mingling of the races isn't wise, especially as she lets herself go into the extremist manifestations of Harlemania torso-twisting and gyrations. It may hurt her personally."[23]

Stepin Fetchit's sad career may be taken as a barometric index of the period. In 1930 he was a hero to many blacks, as a result of appearing in a handful of stylized burlesques of southern Negroes and their responses to racial etiquette. But by 1936 his career at Fox came to an end after a flurry of roles in Will Rogers's

21. The films are in 16-mm release. For journalistic reviews and comment, see *Variety*: May 16, 1929, p. 4; October 9, 1929, pp. 31, 34; April 16, 1930, p. 23; August 27, 1930, pp. 4, 14–15; September 10, 1930, p. 17; July 16, 1930, p. 15; *New York Times*: March 10, 1929; September 5, 1930. See also Cripps, *Slow Fade to Black*, chapter 11.

22. Van Vechten to Johnson, June 26, 1927, James Weldon Johnson Collection, Yale University.

23. August 4, 1937, p. 18. The scene was directed by Vincente Minnelli, without credit. In 1943 he directed MGM's *Cabin in the Sky*.

rural local colorist films, *Judge Priest, The County Chairman, David Harum*, and *Steamboat Round the Bend*. Thenceforward, he slumped into B pictures, short films, and eventually "race movies," having fallen victim to increasingly urbane tastes that did not include the excessive sycophancy that had marked older Negro roles.

This mid-decade burst of Negro activity must not be taken as a revolution in racial attitudes. A glance at the script of Paramount's *So Red the Rose* (1935) is instructive. A high moment comes when Cato, a rebellious slave modeled, it was said, on Nat Turner, harangues the slaves. But the script merely instructs the extras to "laugh like school children released from school" and set upon Cato "laughing like imbecilic animals." When a house servant helps put down the insurrection, he is seen as "loyal and righteous" and "wearing the pride of his race upon his features." Cato can only whine abjectly: "I just a slave nigger that don't know nuthin'."[24]

If the racial temper of the times had changed in ways that would make *The Green Pastures* seem slightly antique, Connelly too had matured and grown settled. In the years since the opening of the play, he had become a resident wit, an elder statesman of the theater, and even a professor in the Yale drama school, all of which helped mold Connelly into an established and lionized figure with a diminished concern for innovation.

Warner Brothers shared the mood as though seeking to produce a "prestige" film that would neither disappoint nor challenge its audience, who would see the movie as a replica of the play they had seen six years earlier. "It was a disappointment to me; I wanted to make it down south; I wanted to do it out of doors," Connelly recalled. "I had an idea of making it into a picture, not to transcribe the play onto film, which was what the Warner Brothers wanted."[25]

Despite Connelly's wishes, his own training and experience in the theater prevailed and the film retained a striking theatrical quality. Most changes from script to screenplay, even those that

24. Script in Doheny Library, University of Southern California. Interview with King Vidor, by telephone, spring 1970.
25. Connelly interview.

heightened its visual quality, were strategic decisions in favor of theatrical, as opposed to cinematic, effects. God's entrances, for example, are always appropriately quiet and simple rather than accompanied by peals of special effects thunder-and-lightning. Even the central episode of Genesis is conveyed by acting rather than special effects, except for a simple camera-stop insertion of Eve into the scene. Those sequences in which secular sin is depicted are carried almost entirely by the actors' flair and personae, assisted by effective costumes rather than self-conscious cinematic devices. Visual rhetoric and embellishment were restricted to the main titles, various special effects that enhanced the biblical deluge, and other "exteriors." The price of such visual augmentation included minor matters, such as the loss of a certain amount of local color, picturesque debates over the merits of minnows and worms as fish bait, a ceremonial awarding of Sunday school diplomas, as well as major losses in theological foundations that had given political meaning and thrust to the stage play.

Unintentionally, Warner Brothers and Connelly reinforced each other in making *The Green Pastures* into a well-made photographed play. No matter how much he wished to make a movie from his script, Connelly's psyche was rooted in theater from earliest childhood. For the Warner brothers' part, the production of a "prestige" classic imported from Broadway dictated that the play come to the screen with few changes. In a candid moment, Connelly remembered the Warners, Harry and Jack, as "terrified people [who] were afraid of originality," and "money men" interested mainly in Connelly's ability to bring in the negative under its $800,000 budget and return an estimated three or four million dollars.[26]

At every turn, the studio appeared to allow Connelly his head while denying him such wishes as the location shooting that might have opened up the action. In the end, he felt the studio regarded the project as a routine film beset by the "cheap" decision of the Warners to lease studio space from themselves. The arrangement so "handicapped the production" that Connelly "hated it" because it grew into a mere "stencil" of his stage play.

26. Connelly interview.

Warners capped its parsimony by releasing the film in the dog days of summer, earning the polite praise reserved for "classics." *Variety's* review, written by editor Abel Green himself, found the movie "a credit to Warner Bros., and the entire motion picture industry,"[27] a tribute as hollow as finding Joe Louis a credit to his race. Connelly muted his disappointment behind press releases praising the studio for its "cooperation."[28]

The press books also played up *The Green Pastures* for its prestige as a long-running American classic in the tradition of *Uncle Tom's Cabin*, *Abie's Irish Rose*, and *Rip Van Winkle*. As though its audience was a respectable, informed, white middle class capable of perceiving black folk-religion with a cultural relativity that might have been acquired through reading the then popular anthropology of Ruth Benedict's *Patterns of Culture*, the ad copy stressed the rich simplicity of "primitive" religion.

Along with the usual tie-ins with department stores and radio programs, Warners' press books encouraged testimony from "lecturing friends," society-page writers, a local "big shot" who had seen the play, and clergymen, providing they were handled "with kid gloves." In the schools, pupils were the targets of a campaign complete with a sixteen-page study guide that tied the movie to the studio's own classics—*A Midsummer Night's Dream* and *Anthony Adverse*.

No "race angle" intruded. In Harold Cox III's illustrations, the actors can barely be taken for Negroes and are never identified as to race. Not until page nineteen did press releases take up the superstitions and dialect of "dusky angels." Even then racial references were disguised by such euphemisms as "the aborigines of Louisiana's bayou." Only as the plot is told at the end, does the exhibitor see clearly the racial identity of the motion picture he is about to put on the market. The capsule narrative opens: "A dozen pickaninnies . . . "

To the dismay of black professionals, the press releases charac-

---

27. July 22, 1936, p. 17.

28. Connelly's recollections vary, perhaps depending on his mood, from resigned patience with the Hollywood system to snappish remembrances of its eternal attention to money, its "banker's eye for percentages." See note 8 for various sources.

terized several of the actors as fey, winsome amateurs. Ida For-
syne is "discovered" dusting and running an elevator in a New
York store; Abraham Gleaves is Connelly's porter on the Santa Fe
Chief on a journey to the West Coast; and so on. In Rex Ingram's
case, the copywriters used a reverse strategy that eventually embarrassed the actor by presenting him as an urban version of the
self-sacrificing agronomist George Washington Carver. Ingram,
according to the story, was born on the Mississippi steamer *Robert
E. Lee*, earned a Phi Beta Kappa key at Northwestern, took a medical doctorate, and turned away from a career as a surgeon only
after his hands were crushed by a trunk lid. Such paragons of
accuracy as the *New York Times* were taken in by many of the
stories, and only *Time* magazine exposed Ingram's overblown autobiography. Most newspapers ran the stories as uncritical rein-
forcement of the popular acceptance of the Negro as a natural
actor whom Connelly had merely provided opportunity.

Reaction to the Film

As though taking their cue from the press books, the nation's
white magazines lavished praise on the movie. *Time* led off with
a spread of ten stills and a recounting of *The Green Pastures*'s phe-
nomenal success on the road, predicting with faint praise that it
should do well in the same medium-sized cities that had enjoyed
the road show. *Literary Digest* and *Canadian Magazine* lifted from
the whole cloth of the press book such tales as the casting from
the ranks of Pullman porters and a synopsis of "the modern
Southern Negro conception of heaven" complete with "pickaninnies." Most of them, like *Commonweal's* James P. Cunningham,
praised its broad range from tragedy to "honest negro humor."
Those magazines that were unenthusiastic, like the educational
trade paper *Scholastic* and the leftist *Nation*, remained neutral or
carped at its constricted mise-en-scène caused by translating a
play from stage to screen. The daily press, typified by the *New
York Times*, praised the film makers for embalming an American
classic on film, holding each detail up to the light and comparing
it with its dramatic source or assaying each cinematic device according to its faithfulness to the original conception. If the reviewer had cause for regret it was only that Rex Ingram's roles as

God, Adam, and Hezdrel were made possible by the death of Richard B. Harrison.[29]

The Green Pastures elicited an even more deeply felt approbrium from the Afro-American press, including the many regional papers whose readers had never seen the play but who read criticism of the arts in the form of "boiler plate" sent out to provincial papers by the Associated Negro Press. Its often effusive praise and its transparent efforts to spur racial pride maximized the impact of *The Green Pastures* and minimized its flaws.

The black press was a longtime voice of the literate, churched, socially and politically affiliated black middle class. As such, it enthusiastically retailed to blacks the myths of American aspiration, personal worth, and success. Such stories included J. A. Rogers's chauvinistic columns on the successful figures from history whom he considered "black": Cleopatra, Hannibal, Abraham Lincoln, and Warren Harding; America's largest black bank or first black millionaire; and the frequent obituaries that began with slavery and ended with prosperity, all of which taught readers a bedrock faith in the American sense of fair play that promised soon to extend to Afro-Americans. In the 1930s, success in Hollywood became a variant on the legend in the form of well-photographed parties, friendships with white stars, long-nosed automobiles, and escapades in usually all-white preserves such as Los Angeles hotels. At first, the reportage merely acknowledged jobs won by armies of black bit-players and extras or, in fan magazines, the careers of Stepin Fetchit or Hattie McDaniel, but after 1930 the stories took up instances of black penetration into the ranks of assistant directors, script doctors, and confidants of the Hollywood elite.

As *The Green Pastures* went into production, it provided the black press with supplemental nutrients that fed the legend. The *Pittsburgh Courier's* theater pages, with a readership that extended through the Ohio and Mississippi valleys, ran many such stories.

29. *Time*, June 29, 1936, pp. 38–40; *Literary Digest*, July 18, 1936, pp. 18–19; *Canadian Magazine*, August 1936, pp. 34–36; James P. Cunningham, "Green Pastures," *Commonweal*, June 5, 1936, p. 160; *Scholastic*, September 19, 1936, p. 17; "Marc Connelly—Moving Man," *Nation*, July 25, 1936, p. 110; *New York Times*, March 8 and July 17, 1936. Also *Variety*, October 23, 1935, p. 8.

Early preproduction stories played up veteran actor George Randol's duties as assistant director and Hall Johnson as musical director. As casting got under way, black reporter Bernice Patton plugged each lucky actor who won a role. Rex Ingram served both sides of the legend: admired as a medical scholar, yet chided as a rake caught in the snares of paternity suits, bigamy, sexual escapades, and bankruptcy.[30]

Each new film release promised a cycle of imitators. *The Green Pastures* was no exception: Patton predicted that "with the screening of 'Green Pastures' a cycle of Biblical folklore with a Negro cast is on." Already, she reported, Randol and Johnson had been signed by RKO; Billy Rowe, a *Courier* writer, heard that Warners planned a musical set in the Cotton Club; and another report touted Connelly as a likely maker of a movie on the Haitian revolution.[31]

At least one black group, Claude Barnett's Associated Negro Press, tried to use the production as a means of advancing the cause of the blacks in Hollywood. The ANP's movie correspondent, Fay M. Jackson, was among the first black reporters to notice the difference between accommodating Hollywood Negroes and more socially conscious New York black actors. When the major roles went to the politically conscious Rex Ingram, she described him to Barnett as an interloper "to whom all the smokes [in Hollywood] object." One of the stories she filed charged the studio with not only stinting on black salaries but employing Connelly as a kind of white straw boss who succeeded because he knew "how to handle Negroes," an account that brought forth an outraged denial from the studio.[32]

Thus the success myth was applied to the Hollywood experi-

30. *Pittsburgh Courier*, January 18, January 25, February 8, March 7, and March 14, 1936; *Afro-American* (Baltimore), August 22, 1936.

31. *Pittsburgh Courier*, June 20 and August 29, 1936. Even those older regional papers reduced by poverty to four-page formats, such as the *Cleveland Gazette*, ran occasional photographs as "teasers," although they had no space for lengthy press book copy. See also *Norfolk Journal and Guide*, February 15, 1936, for pre-release copy.

32. "Fear 'Green Pastures' New Yorkers May Spoil Hollywood," mimeographed press release; Edward Selzer, Warner Brothers, to Jackson, copy, February 3, 1936; Jackson to Barnett, January 15, 1936, Barnett Papers, Chicago Historical Society.

ence in a way that promised a glowing future—both professionally and politically—to black performers. In reporting on preproduction activities, most of the black press played yet another angle that flattered the urban black bourgeoisie and affirmed their social values by contrasting them with the lowly state of the Negroes depicted in *The Green Pastures*. They described the film as a reverent work that "symbolizes the simple and childlike beliefs of many untutored Negroes," thereby paying tribute to their own rise from slavery and poverty.[33]

Only one preproduction story spoiled the ritual: Fay Jackson's report of discriminatory pay scales that threatened to grow into a scandal. But most of the black press headed off the story by accepting the studio's defense, either by quoting unrefuted statements by executives or by reporting from the point of view of Oscar Polk, who played Gabriel in the movie. Polk, a trained and accomplished professional, pointed to his own good pay as a sign of the blacks' well-being. Fortunately for the production, if not the black actors, the newspapers gave the studio the benefit of the doubt.[34]

When the movie appeared, the black press urged it upon its readers as an important cultural event and a monument to black fortitude. Earl J. Morris, who covered Detroit for the *Courier*, exemplified the enthusiasm. "See Warner Brothers' screen classic, 'The Green Pastures,'" he wrote. "It is highly entertaining. . . . The divine comedy will live for years. Marc Connelly did a good job. . . . Rex Ingram stands out in his role of De Lawd . . . but you will love his fighting characterization of Heddrel [sic]" (August 8, 1936). Of all the critics, Morris understood Hezdrel and saw him as a symbol of the new Negro temper. Throughout the

---

33. In still other stories, black newspapers such as the *Gary American* (November 1, 1935) linked achieving blacks with white symbols of success. One story reported that the blackface singer Al Jolson had been put forth as a candidate for the role of God, while another rumor held that *The Green Pastures* would be shot in Technicolor as a hedge against the box-office failure that was "the curse which has befallen all pictures with exclusive Negro casts" (*Norfolk Journal and Guide*, February 15, 1936).

34. *Norfolk Journal and Guide*, February 15, 1936. Earl J. Morris reported from another angle that Ingram's pay for his three key roles came to a mere eight thousand dollars. See *Pittsburgh Courier*, August 8, 1937.

land, the regional black press echoed his encomiums, filled columns with press book copy, and wrote headlines like that in the *Norfolk Journal and Guide*: " 'The Green Pastures' Achieves Immortality and Fulfillment in Its Depiction on the Screen."

Two urban newspapers took sharp issue with the black fans of *The Green Pastures*: the Baltimore *Afro-American*, which reached black communities from South Carolina through New Jersey, and the *Amsterdam News*, which spoke to blacks in Greater New York. Although both papers found much to be desired, the *Afro's* review caused more dismay among distributors because the show business trade paper *Variety* ran a summary of it along with an assertion that *The Green Pastures* had received the worst review in the *Afro's* history. Ralph Matthews, the *Afro's* man, caught the film in Radio City Music Hall remote from Baltimore's segregated houses, and pronounced it a disgrace to Hollywood and to Negroes and a shoestring production little different from those of the "race movie" maker Oscar Micheaux. The blow was only slightly softened when *Variety* checked the story and found that in northern cities blacks had given the film a friendly reception. A week later the *Afro* ran a story from Chicago that minimized the worst and judged the film as merely "an interesting and entertaining spectacle with a cast of underpaid colored actors portraying Marc Connelly's conception of Roark Bradford's impression of unlearned earlier-day beliefs."[35]

Roi Ottley in the *Amsterdam* took up deeper issues, perhaps in keeping with the interests of his urbane audience. Under a characteristically flippant bannerline—" 'Green Pastures' Is Punk"— Ottley not only sneered at the acting, pacing, direction, haste, studio parsimony, muddy make-up, and "amateurish" photography, but also blasted the friendliness with which Negro critics customarily regarded white attempts to render black life on stage and screen. Although the *Amsterdam*, perhaps to mollify advertisers, also ran an ANP piece headlined "Praise Certain for Pastures," Ottley came back with a second attack on Negro critics of the film who, in his view, were corrupted by their urge to praise

35. *Variety*, July 29, 1936, p. 12; *Afro-American*, August 8, 1936; *Amsterdam News*, May 30 and June 6, 1936, A. A. Schomburg Collection, New York Public Library.

any well-meaning white treatment of black life, no matter how shabbily done. *"The Green Pastures* will no doubt, receive magnificent and glowing accounts in the Negro press . . . and unhappily so for the Negro public," he wrote. "Negro newspapers on the whole have a false sense of values. . . . They seem to work from the premise that any time a Negro appears in a play or picture which the whites have produced it should be applauded regardless of its merits."[36] Such patronizing praise, he claimed, corrupted more than it cultivated art.

The box-office success of *The Green Pastures* is more difficult to assess than its critical reception. Connelly recalled that he had brought in the film under the $800,000 that had been budgeted as a negative cost. If he is correct in remembering that it grossed "three or four million dollars," then the movie version of his play earned a profit of perhaps two million. Yet *The Green Pastures* started no trend. Despite the outward signs of success, Hollywood executives were chary of controversial films, especially those with racial themes. They believed that no matter what the merits of the film, it stood to lose the box-office grosses of the South and the small towns that often carried films into the profit column, thus placing the burden of money making on a handful of large urban markets. Thus even fairly successful all-black films such as *Hallelujah!* and *Hearts in Dixie* rarely inspired cycles or sequels. Indeed, one year after the release of *The Green Pastures*, *Variety* reported that Lew Leslie had almost sold Hollywood on making a movie based on his annual *Blackbirds* revues, "but sales departments of the film companies have stymied at least two deals that were all set to go through . . . because of merchandising qualms."[37]

Despite the black critics and the unclear box-office returns, Connelly had, nonetheless, succeeded in capturing a moment in

36. *Amsterdam News*, May 30, June 6, and June 20, 1936.

37. August 18, 1937, p. 1. Whatever the success of *The Green Pastures*, at least a few black critics predicted that its impact would eventually throttle the threadbare little industry known as "race movies" that manufactured films for exclusively black ghetto audiences. So that even to those blacks who regarded the film as an affirmative accomplishment, it was at the expense of the unstable, shabby, often mediocre, but all-black movie industry. See Cripps, *Slow Fade to Black*, chapters 7 and 12.

American racial history and casting it in bronze. Indeed, he and the black critics may have reached a common ground if he had only been more successful in presenting his apocryphal and militant Hezdrel as a metaphor for increasingly self-conscious and aggressive urban Negroes. Without a clearly defined Hezdrel, Connelly had achieved only the limited goal of building a monument to past black dignities that spoke little to the modern black temper. His hope for the play—"I feel that it is offered as an honest inquiry into man's attempt to find dignity and virtue within himself"—simply offered less to blacks than did the potentially powerful allegorical figure of Hezdrel.[38]

As it was, with God presiding over the heavenly fish fry—the master-scene of the film—Hezdrel's place was correspondingly reduced in scale. Yet, as testimony to his potential social meaning, at least one black critic saw and admired Connelly's half-formed intention. And at least one white critic who saw the same thing needled him for his lapsed "objectivity." Without a powerful Hezdrel, *The Green Pastures* led nowhere, either politically or artistically, inspired no trend, and helped label Connelly a one-play author. Later on, like most monuments to the past, *The Green Pastures* was further distorted by time and spoke little to succeeding generations.

Nevertheless, Connelly had taken an element of Negro religion and reshaped it into a sympathetic portrayal through which whites glimpsed the darker side of their arrogant history, and blacks derived race pride from his sentimental treatment of their culture. If later social changes rendered his achievement old-fashioned, *The Green Pastures* should be judged no more harshly than Daniel Chester French's monumental *Lincoln*, Augustus St. Gaudens's allegorical *Grief*, or Horatio Greenough's toga-clad *Washington*. Monuments are monuments.

It should be said in fairness to *The Green Pastures* that at least some of its latter-day reputation as an icon of the old order may be traced to its use as a shorthand expression used by popular critics when speaking against some other bête noir. In its way it suffered the fate of Harriet Beecher Stowe's Uncle Tom. Created

38. Connelly's estimate, made late in his career, is quoted in Nolan, *Marc Connelly*, p. 84.

as a well-meaning indictment of slavery, Tom came to represent not fortitude in the face of misfortune but blind loyalty in the face of oppression. As early as 1930, when Bishop W. J. Walls attacked popular depictions of Afro-American life as "the jazzy, staccato, expression [and] commercialization of primitive weakness," he included Wallace Thurman's drama *Harlem*, the radio show *Amos 'n' Andy*, the Heywards' *Porgy*, and *The Green Pastures* all in the same broad swath.[39] And when Langston Hughes searched for a metaphor that characterized the end of the Harlem Renaissance, he chose Connelly's play: "The cycle that had charlestoned into being on the dancing heels of *Shuffle Along* now ended in *Green Pastures* with *De Lawd*."[40] Over the years, the reputation of the play took on a life of its own, gradually changing its meaning in the minds of later generations. Through Hezdrel it had promised a militant, hopeful black future; by reputation it seemed an apologist for changelessness.

In later years, Connelly and his advisers did not always understand this changing meaning of *The Green Pastures*. By 1951 a revival on Broadway for an audience made sensitive to the budding civil rights movement closed within a month, an anachronism in the age of social "message movies" and assertive Negroes. In 1957, George Schaefer's television version produced for *Hallmark Hall of Fame*—a series that embalmed "classics" into a bland format suitable for framing the commercials of a manufacturer of sentimental greeting cards—received poor ratings despite Connelly's efforts to "clean up" the writing for the occasion.[41]

---

39. Bishop W. J. Walls, "What About Amos 'n' Andy?" *Abbott's Monthly*, December 1930.

40. Langston Hughes, *The Big Sea: An Autobiography* (New York: Knopf, 1945), p. 334.

41. The best that could be said of it appeared in the trade paper *Scholastic Teacher*: "The Hallmark Hall of Fame further endears itself to the nation's English teachers" (October 11, 1957). For commentary on subsequent productions of the play in other media or in revivals, see Connelly to Barrett H. Clark, Dramatists' Play Service, July 6, 1938; November 12, 1938, in Barrett H. Clark Papers, Yale University; Nolan, *Marc Connelly*, p. 84; Columbia Oral History Project, p. 526; *Scholastic Teacher*, October 11, 1957; *New York Times*, July 31, 1957; Morning Telegraph, March 25, 1959, all clippings in Schomburg Collection.

Introduction

SELECTED BIBLIOGRAPHY

Sources for the study of *The Green Pastures* are widely, almost elusively, scattered, perhaps because its author's reputation as a "one-shot" playwright has discouraged study. Of the materials that have been collected, most are ephemera that shed more light on its reception than its production. Marc Connelly's own papers remain in his possession. The most useful bibliography, now ten years old, is found in Paul T. Nolan, *Marc Connelly*, Twayne's United States Authors Series, no. 149 (New York, 1969). Although Nolan takes up *The Green Pastures*, he devotes his attention to its production on the stage rather than the screen, so we lack a thorough study of the play-as-film.

Nolan's bibliography also neglects the film in favor of a literary and theatrical angle. The most primary of the works is Connelly's own essay, "This Play's the Thing: Green Pastures," *Theatre Magazine* (May 1930), pp. 32–35, 66–70. A treatment of the 1951 revival of the play may be found in Marion Kelley,"Backstage: Marc Connelly Back with Prize Play," *Philadelphia Inquirer*, March 24, 1951, pp. 21, 24, and Ward Morehouse, "Broadway After Dark: Prof Connelly (Yale) Talks of 'Pastures'," *New York Sun*, February 1, 1951, p. 20.

Criticism from a black perspective ranges from the near sycophancy of the weekly press to the biting commentary of recent times. A sensitive contemporary appreciation appears in James Weldon Johnson, *Black Manhattan* (New York: Knopf, 1930), pp. 218–24. Another friendly treatment is in Edith J. R. Isaacs, *The Negro in the American Theatre* (New York: McGrath, 1947), pp. 86–88. More acidly etched judgments appear in Loften Mitchell, *Black Drama: The Story of the American Negro in the Theatre* (New York: Hawthorn, 1967), pp. 95–96; and in Nick Aaron Ford's more scholarly essay, "How Genuine Is *The Green Pastures*," *Phylon* (Spring 1960), 67–70. In Doris E. Abramson, *Negro Playwrights in the American Theatre, 1925–1959* (New York: Columbia University Press, 1969), *The Green Pastures* receives scattered attention as a kind of antithesis of genuine black drama. More general comment may be found in Brooks Atkinson, *Broadway* (New York: Macmillan, 1970), pp. 238 ff., and in Nolan's bibliography, along with a selection of uniformly favorable reviews and two of Nolan's own essays on the play.

By way of contrast, the journalistic sources are seemingly infinite. In addition to the accounts, reviews, appreciations, biographical sketches, and gossip that may be found in the *New York Times Index* and the *Readers' Guide to Periodical Literature* volumes for the 1930s, several collections of clippings and other ephemera are available. *The Green Pastures* is disappointingly represented in the James Weldon Johnson Collection in the Beineke Library at Yale, although there are a few reviews and some fugitive letters in the manuscripts of William Lyon Phelps, Frederick B. Millett, and Barrett H. Clark. A small cache of clippings is in the George P. Johnson Collection at the Research Library of the University of California at Los Angeles; a microfilm copy of the collection is on deposit in, among other libraries, the Soper Library of Morgan State University. Volume 33 of the L. S. Alexander Gumby Collection in the Butler Library of Columbia University is devoted to *The Green Pastures*, as is a folder in the vertical file of the A. A. Schomburg Collection in the

New York Public Library. The New York Public Library Performing Arts Collection has *The Green Pastures* ephemera in individual collections, all of which are accessible through cross-indexing under the title of the play. Among them are the Laurence Rivers scrapbooks and the Vandamm Collection. Included among the items are clippings, photographs, posters, souvenir programs, scrapbooks, press books, television studio floor plans, and copies of much of the more ambitious journalistic coverage such as that in *London Mercury*, *Theatre Magazine*, the French language *Correspondant*, *Vanity Fair*, *Theatre Arts*, *Creative Reading*, and many regional and racial serials.

Connelly's own testimony appears in fragmentary form in several places. Nolan quotes from apparently lengthy interviews between Connelly and himself. In the Oral History Collection of Columbia University there is an interview between Connelly and Robert C. Franklin recorded in March 1959. My interview with Connelly on April 15, 1978, is recorded on tape. Connelly has never taken seriously the writing of a thoroughgoing autobiography, but he has turned out *Voices Offstage: A Book of Memoirs* (New York: Holt, Rinehart, and Winston, 1968), which is far more informative about his years among the Algonquin wits than it is on his Hollywood tenure.

1. The low angle and geometrically lighted ceiling in this early scene were among the few consciously cinematic devices.

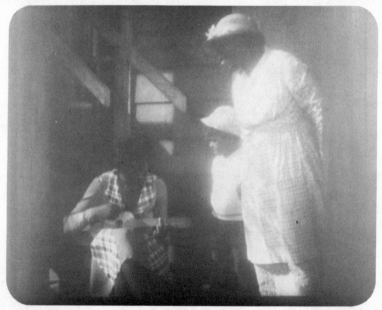

2. Connelly establishes the difference between respectables and riffraff—between virtue and sin—as a choice between sacred and secular music, as in scenes 8–9 when the girl chooses between church and ukulele.

3. Connelly establishes that Negro folk-religion, as presented to children, derives myths from such cultural data as juvenile books and circus posters.

4. Mr. Deshee (George Reed), whose Sunday school opened the play, does not appear in the film until scene 23, having given way to the expository scenes of southern black life.

5. The master shot from which God's presence derived its strength was this ensemble of the entire heavenly host.

6. As comic relief, Connelly prescribed bits of business that included "two buck angels" whose fishing is interrupted by a cherub whose highly mobile cloud is "bumpin' into ev'a'thin'."

7. God (Rex Ingram) partakes of "b'iled custud," a neat analog to the Christian eucharist in its combining symbols of nutrients and holiness.

8. God leaves heaven, his authority underlined by a low-angle shot, to examine the "good earth" he has created and to consider whether "maybe I ought to have somebody to enjoy it."

9. In this double image, one of the characteristically simple special effects, Rex Ingram plays both Adam and God.

10. God's office has an ethereal, clean-lined quality that departs from Connelly's original intention of a cluttered, country-lawyer ambience. Gabriel (Oscar Polk) serves as a kind of executive secretary.

11. *To avoid stereotyping black criminality, the life of riffraff is summed up in a single truck shot along a sin-wracked street.*

12. *The deluge is foreshadowed for Noah (Eddie Anderson) when he gets a twinge in his knee. Thus the grand moments of Judeo-Christian theology are held within the perimeter of familiar southern folklore.*

13. *Like other such incidents, a street stabbing is done in a flash to avoid lingering on what might be taken as specifically black crime.*

14. *"Every dollar was on the screen" in the nevertheless obviously low-budget deluge. The imagery echoes the menagerie in the circus poster early in the film, a familiar bestiary reference source for rural southerners.*

15. In keeping with Protestant theology that places mankind in personal touch with God, the audience sees him from the viewpoint of two cleaning women.

16. The central figure that links Afro-American and Jewish theology is Moses, who led the Hebrew people out of bondage. Moses (Frank Wilson) is seen as an Everyman, a dirt farmer doing God's work.

17. *Moses and Aaron (David Bethea) learn to pass the miracle—changing a rod into a snake—that will win a favor from Pharaoh.*

18. *Pharaoh's court represents Connelly's deepest penetration into black life; it is like a Negro fraternal order at its ceremonial peak.*

19. *The exodus out of Egypt is done mostly as a populist epic, like the passing parade under the titles of* The March of Time.

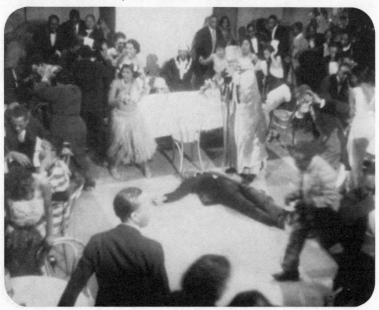

20. *In a dance hall where "the decorations are the gaudy, ugly attempts at elegance one would find in such a place," a prophet (Clinton Rosamond) is killed because he is not "broad-minded" (not in step with modern times).*

21. *The limited budget has already been spent on the deluge. Therefore the climactic battle takes place off camera, with a few sound effects.*

22. *Hezdrel (Ingram) is modern man of the New Testament, active in his own behalf but with faith in God's mercy. He defends Jerusalem, sees to his own wounded, and only incidentally prays.*

23. Hezdrel tells God, who has lost faith in mankind, that mercy is more important than wrath, a lesson learned "through sufferin'."

24. "You has got faith," says God. "Even if dey do lick you tomorrow, I'll bet de Lawd will be waitin' fo' you." And Hezdrel leads the Hebrew people into battle for the Lord.

25. *The angels look over the rim of paradise and see the crucifixion, the final link between Hebrew lore and black Protestant fundamentalism.*

26. *"The sun comes out again, and heaven is radiant." Judeo-Christian lore, as applied to Afro-Americans, has served as a vehicle for a well-made play at the end of which hope is held out for the human condition.*

The Green Pastures

Screenplay

by

MARC CONNELLY

The Green Pastures

Clouds appear before the main title, with the voices of the choir singing "City Called Heaven" coming over. The two cleaning women from God's office start pushing aside the clouds. Down in one corner of the screen a small mortal child watches them. As the clouds roll back, the main title appears. The letters of the words "The Green Pastures" apparently are of metal, and as the first cleaner continues to push the clouds aside, the second cleaner starts flicking the dust off and polishing the letters. When the title is perfectly clear, both women are touching up the lettering. The choir continues over the titles, until, toward the end, the singing diminishes and modulates into one church bell, rung in the tempo which will be used by the sexton in the church.[1]

FADE IN

1. EXT. A LITTLE NEGRO CHURCH   LONG SHOT   DAY
    (MINIATURE)

                                          DISSOLVE TO:

2. INT. CORNER OF CHURCH   MED. CLOSE SHOT
    SEXTON AND BOY
    The sexton is ringing the bell. Sitting beside him is a little boy about four, his grandson, holding the old man's watch.

3. INSERT   CLOSE-UP   WATCH
    in the little boy's hand. It reads three o'clock.

4.   CLOSER SHOT   SEXTON AND GRANDSON
The little boy looks at the watch, fascinated by it. He holds it to his ear. We see the sexton smiling at him. CAMERA MOVES UP TO:

5.   CLOSE SHOT   SEXTON AND GRANDSON

GRANDSON:
Why do dey call dis a watch?

SEXTON:
Caize it watches.

GRANDSON:
It ain't got no eyes.

SEXTON:
Don't need none. We look at *it*. An' it tells us de time.

GRANDSON:
How did it tell you to ring de bell?[2]

SEXTON:
It look up at me an' say: "Don' you think it's time fo' de chillun to come to Sunday school?"

The little boy stares at the watch again and speaks to it:

GRANDSON:
Hello— (He puts the watch to his ear and looks up at the sexton.) It jes' say: "Tick-tick-tick."

The little boy starts to shake the watch.

SEXTON:
Dat mean he want to go back in Gran'py's pocket.[3]

He continues ringing the bell and reaches for the watch.

6.   INT. NEGRO CABIN   MED. CLOSE SHOT AT TABLE
This cabin will later suggest Noah's house. The SOUND of the church bell comes over the scene. Mr. Deshee, the preacher, is finishing a hearty dinner. Seated at the table

about him are: Leon Randall, about forty-five, his host; Mrs. Randall; an old woman relative; and Carlisle, a little boy of seven, who is still eating.

DESHEE:
Well, dat's de best Sunday dinner since I was yere las' time. Only dat bell could pry me from de table.

He rises, as do the others, except Carlisle.

MRS. RANDALL:
You gotta come ag'in soon, Mr. Deshee.

OLD WOMAN (she has not heard Mrs. Randall):
Come ag'in soon.

DESHEE (to Carlisle):
Want to walk to school wid me, Carlisle?

CARLISLE (swallowing a few more mouthfuls):
Yes, suh.

RANDALL:
Maybe by now his stummick too big to tote.

CARLISLE (smiling):
I kin tote it.

MRS. RANDALL (to Carlisle):
Wipe you mouf off.

7. MED. CLOSE SHOT   PROHACK CABIN
Through the open doorway of another cabin we see a little girl of seven adjusting her hat before a broken mirror. The music of the bell has now stopped. She glances away from the mirror.

LITTLE GIRL:
Hurry up wid Carlotta.

We PAN TO a woman of thirty who is spreading wide the bow of a sash tied behind a little girl of five. The little girl herself is spreading the bow of a sash on a little doll.

MRS. PROHACK:
    She all ready.

8.   EXT. ANOTHER CABIN   MED. CLOSE SHOT
We see a girl of seventeen. She is pretty and flashily
dressed. She is idly picking the strings of a ukulele. A
woman's voice comes over the scene:

WOMAN'S VOICE:
    Every Sunday you cain't take him caize you ain't got
    de dishes done! You call dat gittin' de dishes done
    what you doin'? (The girl pays no attention.) Now,
    you hold still, Randolph.

9.   CLOSE SHOT   WOMAN AND LITTLE BOY ENTERING THE
SCENE
The girl's mother is holding the hand of an elaborately
dressed little boy of three. He has a small rubber ball in
his hand.

WOMAN (to the girl):
    Dat's goin' to break yo' min' down.[4]

Disgusted, she leads the little boy past his sister, CAMERA
PANNING WITH THEM.

WOMAN (calling):
    Mis' Prohack!

10.   MED. SHOT   AT DOORWAY OF PROHACK CABIN
The mother of the two little girls comes to the doorway of
her cabin, which is next door.

MRS. PROHACK:
    Hello?

11.   CLOSE SHOT   RANDOLPH'S MOTHER

RANDOLPH'S MOTHER:
    Kin Viney an' Carlotta take Randolph wid dem?

12.   CLOSE SHOT   MRS. PROHACK

MRS. PROHACK:
   Shoo him ovah.

She exits into her cabin.

13.   CLOSE SHOT   RANDOLPH AND HIS MOTHER

RANDOLPH'S MOTHER:
   You go ahead an' behave yo'self like a citizen today.
   (Calling.) Heah he come.

She pats his behind and sends him along.

14.   MED. SHOT   AT DOOR OF PROHACK CABIN
Viney springs from the cabin and surprises Randolph
into a squeal of delight. She hangs on to him and calls
over her shoulder:

VINEY:
   Come on, Carlotta.

Carlotta with her doll comes from the house, and the
three children move off.

15.   EXT. RIVERBANK   MED. CLOSE SHOT
THREE ROUSTABOUTS
lying on some sandbags that have been piled up on the
riverbank to offset a recent flood. One man is lighting a
cigarette. The other two are sprawled on their backs, their
caps pulled over their eyes to keep out the sunlight.

FIRST ROUSTABOUT:
   Did you go ovah to N'Orleans ag'in las' night?

MAN WITH CIGARETTE:
   I was dancin' in de barrelhouse to six o'clock dis
   mo'nin'. I'm goin' ovah ag'in tonight.

ZUBO:
   You is a river-crossin' fool.

Mr. Deshee and Carlisle walk into scene. Mr. Deshee looks disapprovingly at the three men.

MAN WITH CIGARETTE (to third man):
You want to come 'long and git drunk tonight, Zubo?

ZUBO:
I bin wukkin' too hard makin' de Mississippi be- have. My strength ain't back in me yit.

MAN WITH CIGARETTE:
De flood started goin' down Wednesday. You ain't lifted a bag since Wednesday noon. How long you think you gonna need befo' you feel yo'self ag'in?

ZUBO (turning over comfortably):
I ain't yit in a position to say.[5]

16.   CLOSE SHOT   MR. DESHEE AND CARLISLE WALKING
CAMERA TRUCKING BEFORE THEM

CARLISLE:
Is de river gonna rise ag'in, Mr. Deshee?

DESHEE:
No, de weather gonna be fine now. See de pretty clouds ovah dere?

17.   A CLOUD EFFECT, USING CUMULUS CLOUDS

18.   MED. CLOSE SHOT   DESHEE AND CARLISLE WALKING

CARLISLE:
Maybe dey bring mo' rain.

DESHEE:
Not dat kin' of cloud.

CARLISLE:
What good is de clouds like dat, den?

DESHEE:
>   I don' know. Maybe de Lawd jes' use dem fo' sofa pillows.

CARLISLE (laughing):
>   What he do—put his head on dem?

DESHEE:
>   Maybe so.[6]

Carlisle laughs at his own humor, and calls out:

CARLISLE:
>   Hello, Myrtle!

19.   MED. CLOSE SHOT   TWO LITTLE BOYS, A GIRL, AND A VERY SMALL CHILD
The two boys and the girl are about eight. One of the bigger boys has a very little child tied to him by a rope, which is around the child's waist. They are all looking at a circus poster on a billboard that reads:

DRISCOLL'S GREATER CIRCUS

EAST GRETNA, SATURDAY, MAY 6TH

It is an eight-sheet showing wild animal acts.
   Myrtle looks away and waves to Carlisle. We STAY ON the children. One of the little boys is carrying a picture book of animals, and as they continue to speak we see Mr. Deshee and Carlisle entering the SHOT.[7]

FIRST BOY (pointing to tiger on billboard):
>   An' what dat one?

SECOND BOY:
>   Lion.

FIRST BOY:
>   Den what *is* a tiger?

SECOND BOY:
>   Tiger is de lion's wife.

FIRST BOY:

> You don't know, either. (He approaches Mr. Deshee and shows him one of the pictures in his animal book.) Will dey have dat t'ing in de circus, Mr. Deshee?

Mr. Deshee peers down at the book.

20.   INSERT   CLOSE-UP   BOOK
On the top of the page are the letters:
>   "A is for 'Aardvark' "
Below is a picture of an aardvark.

21.   MED. CLOSE SHOT   MR. DESHEE AND CHILDREN

DESHEE:

> If dey do, I want to see it. Come on, we cain't talk 'bout circuses on de Lawd's time. (He hands the book back to the little boy.)

22.   MED. SHOT   DESHEE AND CHILDREN WALKING   CAMERA
TRUCKING WITH THEM
They leave the billboard and continue walking.

MYRTLE:

> What de story goin' to be 'bout today, Mr. Deshee?

MR. DESHEE:

> Ain't goin' to tell a story today. We goin' right to de Good Book itself. You goin' to hear 'bout Genesis.

SECOND BOY:

> What's Genesis, Mr. Deshee?

DESHEE:

> You pick up yo' feet. You find out.

>   DISSOLVE TO:

23.   INT. SUNDAY SCHOOL ROOM   CLOSE SHOT   DESHEE

DESHEE:

> "An' all de days dat Adam lived were nine hund'ed

62

an' thirty years; an' he died. An' Seth lived a hund'ed an' five years an' begat Enos; an' Seth lived after he begat Enos eight hund'ed an' seven years an' begat sons an' daughters. An' all de days of Seth were nine hund'ed an' twelve years; an' he died."

CAMERA PULLS BACK TO:

24.   MED. SHOT   SUNDAY SCHOOL ROOM[8]

We see about twelve children. Their costumes are those that might be seen in any lower Louisiana town at Sunday school time. The children are listening with varied degrees of interest. Three or four are wide-eyed in their attention. Two or three are obviously puzzled, but interested, and the smallest ones are engaged in more physical concerns. Carlotta is playing with her little doll, and Randolph runs his finger on all the angles of his chair. We also recognize Myrtle and the two little boys, and Viney who sits between Carlotta and Randolph in the front row. In the back of the room are sitting the sexton and his little grandson. Deshee continues reading from the Bible.[9]

DESHEE:

An' den it go on like dat till we come to Enoch an' de book say: "An' Enoch lived sixty an' five years an' begat Methuselah." Den it say: "An' all de days of the Methuselah were nine hund'ed an' sixty an' nine years an' he died." An' dat was de ol'est man dat ever was. Dat's why we call ol' Mr. Gurney's mammy ol' Mis' Methuselah, caize she's so ol'. Now, how you think you gonter like de Bible?

MYRTLE:

I think it's jes' wonderful, Mr. Deshee. I cain't understand any of it.

FIRST BOY:

Why did dey live so long, Mr. Deshee?

DESHEE:

Well, dey was mighty men in dem days. But [although] dey was awful mighty, dey always knew God was beyond dem all.

MYRTLE:
What did God look like, Mr. Deshee?

DESHEE:
Well, nobody know, exactly. When I was a little boy, I used to imagine he looked jes' like our ol' preacher, de Reverend Mr. Dubois. He was de wisest an' de finest lookin' man I ever seen.

CARLISLE:
What de worl' look like when de Lawd begin, Mr. Deshee?

DESHEE:
How you mean what it look like?

MYRTLE:
Carlisle mean who was in N'Orleans den.

DESHEE:
Dey wasn't nobody in N'Orleans on 'count dey wasn't any N'Orleans. You got to get yo' minds fixed. Dey wasn't any Canal Street. Dey wasn't any Louisiana. Dey wasn't anythin' on de earth caize fo' de reason dey wasn't any earth. The whole worl' wasn't anythin' at all 'cept a mess of bad weather.

25.   CLOSE-UP   OF THE SEXTON'S GRANDSON
staring straight into the CAMERA. SUPERIMPOSE A SHOT of a terrific thunderstorm (JACKMAN), with trees bending in the wind, perhaps a kitten being drenched. The sound of a hurricane comes over.[10] THE SUPERIMPOSED SHOT FADES OUT, leaving the boy.

26.   MED. CLOSE SHOT   ROOM

MYRTLE:
Yes, but what Carlisle wanter know is—

DESHEE (interrupting and addressing Randolph, who has been playing with his chair and paying no attention):
Now, Randolph, if you don't listen, how you gonter grow up an' be a good man? You wanter to a transgressor?

RANDOLPH (frightened):
No.

DESHEE:
You tell yo'mammy yo' sister got to come wid you nex' time. She kin git de things done in time to bring you to de school. You content yo'self.

The little boy straightens up in his chair.

DESHEE:
Now, what do Carlisle wanter know?

CARLISLE:
How de Lawd decide he want de worl' to be right yere an' how he get de idea he wanted it?

MYRTLE:
Caize de Book say, don't it, Mr. Deshee?

DESHEE:
De Book say, but at de same time dat's a good question. I remember when I was little like you I asked Mr. Dubois de same thing. An' he say: "My son, de Book ain't got time to go into all de details." An' he was right. We don't know jes' where heaven was at, but dere it was. Maybe it was everywhere. Den one day de Lawd say: "Think I'll make me some places." He made de sun an' de moon, de stars. An' he made de earth.

MYRTLE:
Who was aroun' den, nothin' but angels?

DESHEE:
I suppose so.

FIRST BOY:

What was de angels doin' up dere?

DESHEE:

Oh, dey jes' flew aroun' an' had a good time. Dey wasn't no sin, so dey musta had a good time.

ANOTHER BOY:

Did dey have Sunday school too?

DESHEE:

Dey must of had fo' de li'l cherubs.

CARLISLE:

Did dey have picnics?

DESHEE:

Sho, de best kind of picnics. Dey had fish frys, wid b'iled custard an' ten-cent seegars fo' de adults. God give us humans lotsa ideas 'bout good-timin'. Maybe from things he'd seen de angels do. Yes, suh, I bet dey had a fish fry eve'y week. Maybe dey had one eve'y day. Dey wasn't no mankind to worry 'bout yit.

ANOTHER BOY:

Did dey go fishin'?

DESHEE:

Sho, de fishermen fished an' de cooks cooked, an' dey was plenty to eat fo' all. De chillun played, an' de grown-ups passed de time of day. Exceptin' of cose de choir.

27.   CLOSE SHOT   LITTLE BOY

BOY:

What did dey do?

28.   CLOSE SHOT   DESHEE

DESHEE:

God gave dem songs to sing.

29.   A SERIES OF CLOSE-UPS OF THE CHILDREN
with Deshee's voice coming over them.

DESHEE'S VOICE:
So dey sang to de Lawd de songs he liked to hear.

As the CLOSE-UPS continue more rapidly until the faces
become indistinguishable, the voices of the choir come
over the SHOTS, and clouds gradually obscure the scene.

FADE OUT

FADE IN
The voices of the choir are heard very, very softly, gradually growing louder, as we see

[30–33.]EXT. FISH FRY   LONG SHOT FROM A FIFTY-FOOT   DAY
ELEVATION
The SHOT takes in a large sweep of landscape. In the
middle distance, under a clump of live oak, are the par-
ticipants in the scene, wandering about the kettles and
the service tables. They are angels in that they wear
brightly colored robes and have wings protruding from
their backs. Otherwise they look and act like a company
of happy Negroes at a fish fry. As the CAMERA AP-
PROACHES, we see, among the various groups, two women
angels greeting each other delightedly, apparently after a
long absence. A young girl angel and a young man angel
are surrounded by a group. The girl is bashfully and
coyly the target of the good-natured teasing of the others.
The young man, tall, is smiling down at her. His left hand
holds her right hand. Someone cries, "Let's see it! Let's see
it! " She lifts her left hand to show an engagement ring.
In another group, elderly men are selecting cigars. Three
or four amused adults, one with his hand over his mouth,
are looking at a little boy to whom attention has been
called by a mammy angel who stands beside him,
dumbfounded, as she looks at her friends. In the cherub's
mouth is a big cigar. He is strutting.
Part of the scene is momentarily obscured by the pas-

sage of small billowy clouds. At one side perhaps a hundred other Negroes are marching in pairs, singing. As the CAMERA CONTINUES approaching downward toward the center of the scene, it passes a cloud (not solid) that has been masked earlier in the scene by the other clouds. On this cloud, which is like a heroic-size sofa pillow, two buck angels are fishing, their lines attached to homemade fish poles which extend over the side of the cloud. Sailing swiftly into the SHOT is a tiny cloud that a nine-year-old cherub is motivating by his wings. It collides with the larger cloud.

FIRST FISHERMAN:
What you tryin' to do?

CHERUB (pleasantly):
I'm bumpin' into ev'a'thin'.[11]

CAMERA CONTINUES DOWN AND STOPS IN:

MONTAGE SHOTS   FISH FRY

1. After the LONG APPROACH SHOT, the man cook walks upstage to the group in which the woman cook is dipping a fish in cracker dust. As she carries it toward the pot, she goes into the "Fishin' wid worms! " scene.

2. Baby in the brook scene. A small cherub has fallen into the brook.

3. Elderly men are selecting cigars. Behind them the angel pushes the cherub on the swing.

4. Another angle of the cigar boxes. A baby has got into them and is holding one of the cigars in his mouth as he struts. The angel on the swing is behind.

5. Scene 36 MED. SHOT   MAMMY ANGEL LOOKING FOR FITZHUGH.

6. The young engaged couple.

7. Three or four cherubs screaming with laughter as they are being chased by one who is blindfolded. The angel on the swing in the background.[12]

The Sunday school cherubs will come in in front of the CAMERA downstage, by the planking over the stream.

34.   CLOSE SHOT   COOKS NEAR TABLE
A woman cook is looking at the fishermen.

WOMAN COOK:
>   Fishin' wid worms! Fishin' wid worms! Minny fishin'
>   is de only kin' of fishin'!

MAN COOK:
>   Sister, worms is de only thing fo' catfishin'. De trouble
>   is, you got minny fishin' on de brain.

WOMAN COOK:
>   Go right on, loud mouf. You tell me de news. My,
>   my! You jes' de wisest person in de distric'. Fust you,
>   den de Lawd God. [13]

35.   CLOSE-UP   MAN COOK
He is speechless, helpless.

36.   MED. SHOT   GROUP AT TABLE
They have been amused by the argument, which has interrupted their selection of tidbits from the table. They
resume eating. A distracted mammy angel enters the
scene.

MAMMY ANGEL:
>   Anybody yere seen Fitzhugh?

WOMAN ANGEL:
>   A minute ago he was up in de element.

The mammy angel looks up.

37.   CLOSE SHOT   CHERUB ON CLOUD
The "Indian" is now standing on one foot on his cloud,
the other foot in the air, arms extended, more or less like
a bareback rider in the circus.

38.   CLOSE-UP   MAMMY ANGEL'S FACE

MAMMY ANGEL:
>   You fly down yere! Now you heerd me, Fitzhugh.

You wanter be put down in de sin book? (She reaches for a glass of boiled custard.) Dat baby must got imp blood in him he so vexin'. (Looking up again.) You want me to fly up dere an' slap you down?

39.   MED. CLOSE SHOT   ANOTHER GROUP
A fat angel is lightly but firmly tapping the back of a three-year-old cherub. The baby has the better part of an enormous catfish sandwich in her hand.

STOUT ANGEL:
    I tol' you you was too little fo' catfish.

A slender angel enters the scene. She is daintily eating a dripping sandwich.

SLENDER ANGEL:
    What de trouble wid Leonetta?

STOUT ANGEL:
    She got a catfish bone down her froat. (Continuing to tap.) Doggone, I tol' you to eat grinnel instead.

SLENDER ANGEL:
    Ef'n she do eat all dat, she gonter get de bellyache.

STOUT ANGEL:
    Ain't I tol' her? (To the cherub.) Come on now—let-go-dat-*bone!*

As she says "bone," she slaps the cherub's back again.

40.   CLOSE-UP   CHERUB
Reaching in her mouth, she takes out a fish bone and holds it up for approval. She looks up smiling as if she had just done something very clever. Over the SHOT comes the voice of the stout angel:

STOUT ANGEL'S VOICE:
    Dat's good.

41. MED. SHOT GROUP

SLENDER ANGEL:
Now she all right.

STOUT ANGEL (to cherub):
Go on an' play wid yo' cousins.

The cherub skips out of the scene.

STOUT ANGEL (to slender angel):
I ain't see you lately, Lily. How you been?

SLENDER ANGEL:
Oh, fine. I been visitin' my mammy. She been pro-
moted to waitin' on de welcome table over by de
throne of grace.

STOUT ANGEL:
She always was pretty holy.

SLENDER ANGEL:
Yes, ma'am. I guess de Lawd's took quite a fancy to
her.

STOUT ANGEL:
Well, dat's natchel. I declare yo' mammy one of de
finest lady angels I know.

SLENDER ANGEL:
She claim you de best one she know.

STOUT ANGEL:
Well, when you come right down to it, I s'pose we is
all pretty near perfec'.

SLENDER ANGEL (taking another bite of the sandwich):
Yes, ma'am. Why is dat, Mis' Jenny?

STOUT ANGEL:
I s'pose it's caize de Lawd he don' 'low us 'sociatin'
wid de devil any mo' so dat dey cain't be no mo'
sinnin'.

SLENDER ANGEL:
Po' ol' Satan. Whutevah become of him?

STOUT ANGEL:
De Lawd put him someplace I s'pose.

SLENDER ANGEL:
It so happens I do a great deal of travelin', an' I never come across anyplace but heaven anywhere. So, secondly, if de Lawd kick Satan out of heaven jes' whereat did he go? Dat's my question.

STOUT ANGEL:
You bettah let de Lawd keep his own secrets, Lily. De way things is goin' now dey ain't been no sinnin' since dey give dat scamp a kick in de pants. Nowadays heaven's free of sin, an' if a lady wants a little constitutional she kin fly [til] she wing-weary—(she moves her shoulders, making the wings flutter) widout gittin' insulted.

SLENDER ANGEL (pensively):
I was jes' a baby when Satan lef'. I don't even 'member what he look like.

STOUT ANGEL:
Well, he was jes' right fo' a devil.[14]

42.   MED. SHOT   PART OF THE CROWD
through which a tall patriarchal archangel is making his way with a basket containing Sunday school diplomas, each tied with a pretty ribbon. He is very busy looking around for an eminence on which he can stand to give out the Sunday school cards. He is preoccupied rather than rude as he pays little attention to the occasional "good mo'nin's" from those he passes. The CAMERA PANS with him until the stout angel appears in the SHOT.

STOUT ANGEL:
Good mo'nin', Archangel.

72

ARCHANGEL:
> Good mo'nin', folks.

The choir stops.

43. MED. SHOT   SMALL GROUP OF ANGELS NEAR ARCHANGEL

FIRST ANGEL:
> What is it?

SECOND ANGEL:
> De Sunday school class.

44. MED. SHOT   THE CHOIR
It has halted and has stopped singing at the signal of the leader.

45. CLOSE SHOT   ARCHANGEL

ARCHANGEL (to choir):
> You kin keep singin' while I give out de Sunday school cyards.

46. MED. CLOSE SHOT   THE CHOIR
The choir leader snaps an old-time tuning fork and sings the note loudly, at which the choir begins softly to sing "When the Saints Come Marching In."

47. MED. CLOSE SHOT   THE ARCHANGEL
looking off scene.

ARCHANGEL:
> All right, bring 'em yere.

PULL BACK TO:

48. FULL SHOT   PART OF CROWD
As the CAMERA PULLS BACK we see the backs of ten cherubs, five girls and five boys, marching in twos away from the CAMERA. The music of the choir comes over the scene. Walking backwards, as she conducts the march of the cherubs with a stick used as a baton, is a woman teacher-angel. In addition to a conventional robe and wings like

73

those of the other angels, she wears a prim-looking hat and pince-nez. As the children march past the CAMERA into position facing the archangel, we see that they are wearing stiffly starched white suits and dresses, the little girls having enormous ribbons at the backs of their dresses and smaller ones in their hair and on the tips of their small wings. Hurrying to get into the parade is a girl cherub with two small babies about two years old. Their wings are made of maribou. One falls flat on its face and is instantly pulled up by the girl.

49.   MED. SHOT   CHILDREN
in which we see the backs of the children, ranged in two lines with the boys nearer the CAMERA as they face the archangel.

ARCHANGEL:
   Now den cherubs, why is you yere?

50.   REVERSE ANGLE   CLOSE SHOT   CHERUBS

CHERUBS:
   Becaize we so good.

51.   CLOSE SHOT   ARCHANGEL

ARCHANGEL:
   Dat's right. Now who de big boss?

52.   CLOSE SHOT   CHERUBS

CHERUBS:
   Our dear Lawd.

53.   CLOSE SHOT   ARCHANGEL

ARCHANGEL:
   Dat's right. When you all grow up what you gonter be?

CHERUBS:
   Holy angels at de throne of grace.

54. CLOSE SHOT   ARCHANGEL

ARCHANGEL:
Now, you passed yo' 'xaminations and it gives me great pleasure to hand out de cyards fo' de whole class. (He looks at the first diploma.) Gineeva Chaproe.

55. ANOTHER ANGLE   TO INCLUDE THE ARCHANGEL AND CHERUBS
The first girl cherub goes to him and gets her diploma, and instantly dashes out of scene.

ARCHANGEL (taking out second diploma):
Corey Moulter.

The second girl cherub goes up to him. She modestly bites her lip as she receives her diploma.

56. CLOSE SHOT
The first girl cherub, Gineeva Chaproe, hands her diploma to her proud parents, who are among the picnickers. Over the SHOT comes the voice of the archangel:

ARCHANGEL'S VOICE:
Nootzie Winebush.

Gineeva's mother looks at an old man nearby and smiles.

GINEEVA'S MOTHER:
You 'member Gineeva.

OLD MAN:
Which one is it?

ARCHANGEL'S VOICE:
Harriet Prancy.

GINEEVA'S MOTHER (to old man):
Gineeva.

OLD MAN (nodding, completely unimpressed):
Oh, yes.

ARCHANGEL'S VOICE:
Brozain Stew't.

57.   MED. CLOSE SHOT   ARCHANGEL AND BOY CHERUBS
All the little girls have scattered by this time.

ARCHANGEL (to boys):
Now you boys know yo' own names. S'pose you
come yere an' help me git dese 'sorted right?

The boys cluster around him.

58.   MED. CLOSE SHOT   GROUP AROUND GINEEVA
Gineeva's mother's smile fades as a look of pleased sur-
prise comes over her face.

GINEEVA'S MOTHER (muttering softly):
Gabriel!

Gineeva's mother and father and the old man look off
scene in the same direction, also muttering "Gabriel!"
We PAN OVER most of the entire company as everyone
looks off scene in the same direction. On the sound of
"Gabriel" from those nearest them, the voices of the choir,
which has been singing, trail off, and the members of the
choir among themselves murmur "Gabriel! Gabriel!" The
CAMERA CONTINUES TO PAN as the attention of the company is centered upon Gabriel.[15]

MOVE UP TO:

59.   MED. CLOSE SHOT   GABRIEL
Gabriel is bigger and more elaborately winged than even
the archangel, but he is also much younger and beardless.
His costume is less conventional than that of the other
men, resembling more the Gabriel of the Doré drawings.
Gabriel calmly but searchingly looks the assemblage over.
He lifts his hand.

GABRIEL:
Gangway! Gangway fo' de Lawd God Jehovah!

There is a reverent hush.

60.   CLOSE-UP   A MAN ANGEL
brushing the dust off his sleeve.

61.   CLOSE-UP   A WOMAN ANGEL
pressing back the hair over her ears.

62.   CLOSE-UP   A MAMMY ANGEL
giving a quick flip to the wings of a cherub.

63.   CLOSE-UP   A LITTLE GIRL CHERUB
straightening out the necktie of a little boy cherub. (NOTE:
At the end of each CLOSE-UP each figure comes to soldierly
attention, readying itself for its audience.)

64.   FULL SHOT   THE ENTIRE COMPANY   FROM GABRIEL'S
ANGLE
Everyone stands at attention.

65.   CLOSE SHOT   GOD   REVERSE ANGLE
(NOTE: If it can be done without distortion, the CAMERA
POSITION in all the early shots of the Lord should be about
on a level with his knees.) He is standing in front of Gabriel. He is the tallest and biggest of them all. He wears a
white shirt with a white bow tie, a long Prince Albert
coat of black alpaca, black trousers, and congress gaiters.
He looks at the assemblage. There is a pause. He speaks
in a rich, bass voice:

GOD:
    Is you been baptized?

OTHERS' VOICES (over SHOT):
    Certainly, Lawd.

GOD:
    Is you been baptized?

OTHERS' VOICES (over SHOT):
    Certainly, Lawd.

GOD:
Is you been baptized?

OTHERS' VOICES (over SHOT, introducing a melody to their responses):
Certainly Lawd. Certainly, certainly, certainly, Lawd.

GOD (with a faint smile and with the beginning of musical notation):
Is you been redeemed?

66. The CAMERA STARTS TO TRUCK BACK SLOWLY, away from God, regressing through the company, which chants the responses.

OTHERS (half-singing):
Certainly, Lawd.

GOD:
Is you been redeemed?

OTHERS:
Certainly, Lawd.

GOD:
Is you been redeemed?

OTHERS:
Certainly Lawd. Certainly, certainly, certainly, Lawd.

GOD:
Do you bow mighty low?

OTHERS:
Certainly, Lawd.

GOD:
Do you bow mighty low?

OTHERS:
Certainly, Lawd.

The CAMERA NOW COMES TO REST, and we see a

67.   FULL SHOT   PANORAMA OF THE ENTIRE FISH FRY
But in place of the scores who were in the original groups,
there are now hundreds in the company.

GOD:
    Do you bow mighty low?

OTHERS:
    Certainly, Lawd. Certainly, certainly, certainly, Lawd.

As the last response ends, all heads are bowed.

68.   CLOSE SHOT   GOD
He looks at them for a moment, then lifts his hand.

GOD:
    Let de fish fry proceed.

69.   FULL SHOT   THE FISH FRY
The picnickers resume their selection of food and general
informal manner. The choir, however, does not yet start
singing. There is a rush toward the Lord of half a dozen
of the children, the older ones wanting to show him their
diplomas, the smaller ones to play.

70.   MED. CLOSE SHOT   GOD AND CHERUBS
A boy cherub, about five, seizes the Lord's coattail and,
bracing himself against the Lord's shoes, hangs at an
angle, swinging on the coattail. The archangel enters the
scene.

ARCHANGEL:
    Good mo'nin', Lawd.

GOD:
    Good mo'nin', Deacon. You lookin' pretty spry.

71.   CLOSE SHOT   A MAMMY ANGEL
looking off scene. She is embarrassed. Over the SHOT comes
the archangel's voice:

ARCHANGEL'S VOICE:
> I cain' complain. We jes' been givin' out cyards to
> de chillun.

We see the mammy angel dart off through the crowd.

72.   MED. SHOT   GROUP AROUND GOD

GOD:
> Dat's good.

One of the cooks has come into the scene, and offers God
a fish sandwich. God declines politely in pantomime. The
mammy angel enters the scene.

MAMMY ANGEL:
> Now, you leave go de Lawd's coat, Herman. You
> heah me?

73.   CLOSE SHOT   GOD
looking down and smiling at the child.

74.   MED. SHOT   GOD AND GROUP

GOD:
> Dat's all right, sister. He jes' playin'.

He picks up the cherub and spanks him good-naturedly.
The cherub squeals with delight and runs to his disap-
proving mother, who leads him out of the scene. Gabriel
approaches with a glass of custard.[16]

GABRIEL:
> Little b'iled custud, Lawd?[17]

GOD:
> Thank you very kindly. Dis looks nice.

One of the angel attendants has entered and stands on
the other side of the Lord.

ANGEL (offering a box):
> Ten-cent seegar, Lawd?

GOD (selecting one):
Thank you, thank you. How de fish fry goin'?

AD LIB:
Okay, Lawd. Fine an' dandy, Lawd. De best one yit,
Lawd, etc.

GOD (looking off scene and raising his voice):
How you shouters gittin' on?

75. MED. CLOSE SHOT CHOIR

CHOIR LEADER:
We been marchin' an' singin' de whole mo'nin'.

76. MED. CLOSE SHOT GOD

GOD:
I heerd you. You gittin' better all de time. You gittin'
as good as de choir at de throne. Why don' you give
us one dem ol' time jump-ups?

77. CLOSE SHOT CHOIR LEADER

CHOIR LEADER:
Anythin' you say, Lawd. (He turns to the choir.) "So
High!"

PULL BACK TO:

78. FULL SHOT CHOIR
as they begin to sing "So High You Can't Get Over Him."
The music continues softly over the following scenes.

79. MED. SHOT GROUP AROUND GOD
A man angel advances holding a cigar, the ash of which
he politely knocks off. He bows and offers the cigar to the
Lord.

GOD:
No, thanks. I'm gonter save dis awhile.

The group beamingly watches God put the cigar in his
pocket and listen to the singing. God lifts the custard to
his lips and sips. After a second sip, a look of displeasure
comes over his face.

GABRIEL:
What's de matter, Lawd?

GOD (sipping again):
I ain't jes' sure yit. Dey's somethin' 'bout dis cus-
tahd. (Taking another sip.)

A custard maker brushes aside the angel who had offered
the light in a panic of inquiry.

CUSTARD MAKER:
Ain't it all right, Lawd?

GOD (casually):
It don't seem seasoned jes' right. You make it?

CUSTARD MAKER:
Yes, Lawd. I put everythin' in it like I allus do. It's
supposed to be perfec'.

GOD:
Yeah. I kin taste de eggs an' de cream an' de sugar.
(He smiles.) I know what it is. It needs jes' a little bit
mo' firmament. [18]

CUSTARD MAKER (sheepishly):
Dey's firmament in it, Lawd.

GOD:
Maybe, but it ain' enough.

CUSTARD MAKER (suddenly smiling and depending on a
confession):
Well, it's all we had, Lawd. Dey ain't a drap left in
de jug.

GOD:
Dat's all right. I'll jes' r'ar back an' pass a miracle. [19]

80.   MED. CLOSE SHOT   GABRIEL
      raising his hand.

81.   MED. FULL SHOT   CHOIR
      It stops singing.

82.   MED. CLOSE SHOT   GOD AND GROUP
      GOD:
         Let it be some firmament.

      As God speaks, there arises a soft murmuring wind,
      which increases until the end of the speech. The sound of
      the wind should modulate to instrumental orchestration,
      not unlike the "island" music that O'Neill wrote for Bar-
      rie's *Mary Rose*.[20] (NOTE: If the music department is unfa-
      miliar with this music, it can probably be borrowed for
      consultation from the Gilbert Miller office in New York.)

      GOD:
         An' when I say let it be some firmament, I don't want
         jes' a little bitty dab o' firmament caize I'm sick an'
         tired of runnin' out of it when we need it. Let it be a
         whole mess of firmament!

83.   FULL SHOT   THE HEAVENS   (JACKMAN)
      Clouds are gathering into a single formation at a terrific
      speed. As they gather, it grows darker.

84.   CLOSE-UP   GOD
      Now the light has grown very dim.

      GOD:
         Dat's de way I like it.

85.   LONG SHOT   THE ENTIRE ASSEMBLAGE
      in which the figures of the company can be dimly dis-
      cerned in a cloud bank that almost blots out the scene.

AD LIB (over the SHOT):

> Dat's a lot of firmament. My, dat is firmament! Look to me like he's created rain, etc.

86. CLOSE-UP THE HEAD OF A MAMMY ANGEL
just above the cloud. She is looking down.

MAMMY ANGEL:

> Now look, Lawd, dat's too much firmament. De cherubs is gittin' all wet.

87. CLOSE-UP THE TOP OF ANOTHER MAMMY ANGEL'S HAT
above the cloud.

SECOND MAMMY ANGEL:

> Look at my Carlotta, Lawd. She's soaked to de skin. Dat's *plenty* too much firmament.[21]

88. MED. CLOSE SHOT GOD
The mist is around and behind him, and if the CAMERA-MAN himself will kindly work a miracle, we will have the effect of a nimbus. (JACKMAN)

GOD:

> Well, 'co'se we don't want de chillun to ketch cold. Cain't you dreen it off?

GABRIEL'S VOICE:

> Dey's no place to dreen it, lawd.

FIRST MAMMY ANGEL'S VOICE:

> Why don't we jes' take de babies home, Lawd?

GOD:

> No, I don't wanta bust up de fish fry. You angels keep quiet an' I'll pass another miracle. Dat's always de trouble wid miracles. When you pass one you always gotta r'ar back an' pass another.

The wind stops.

GOD:

> Let dere be a place to dreen off dis firmament. Let dere be mountains an' valleys an' let dere be oceans an' lakes. An' let dere be rivers an' bayous to dreen it off in, too. As a matter of fac', let dere be de earth. An' when dat's done let dere be de sun, an' let it come out an' dry my cherubs' wings.

89.   FULL SHOT   THE FISH FRY

The mist clears. The foreground is as it was before, but in the background, instead of an infinity of landscape as before, we see, behind the picnickers and the choir, a rise in the ground, topped by "the golden gates" shining in the sun. The gates themselves resemble in pattern the beautiful wrought iron gates one can still see in the old houses of the French quarter of New Orleans.

The cherubs are being examined by their parents. There is an ad lib murmur:

AD LIB:

> You all right, honey? You feel better now, Albert? Now you all dry, Vangy?

90.   MED. SHOT   GABRIEL

touching and looking at the gates. He looks down over the gates and sees something off scene. An intense light is shining on his face, coming from below. He is astonished and turns back to the assemblage.

GABRIEL (shouting):
> Look heah!

91.   LONG SHOT

The assemblage rushes to the edge of the embankment and peers down excitedly. We see God standing in the foreground alone, facing the CAMERA.

92. FULL SHOT   FROM BELOW   (JACKMAN)
taking in the assemblage looking over the edge of the
embankment.

93. LONG SHOT   THE GLOBE   AS SEEN FROM THE
ASSEMBLAGE   (JACKMAN)
The globe is still spinning in space with the force of its
creation. It slows down quickly, and when it stops we see
that it is the earth. Instead of the conventional continental
and ocean outlines, it is apparently part farming land,
with old wooden fences, clumps of trees, brooks, etc.

94. MED. SHOT   TAKING IN THE BACKS OF THE ASSEMBLAGE,
INCLUDING GABRIEL, WITH THE EARTH IN THE
DISTANCE   (PROCESS)
The following are audible in an ad lib burst of ex-
clamations:

AD LIB:
Dere she is, hot from de oven! Well, I declah! He's
invented roundness! Dey got de order! Now, you
know dat was somethin' to do.

Gabriel turns toward the CAMERA.

GABRIEL:
Do you see it, Lawd?

95. FULL SHOT   THE ASSEMBLAGE, WITH GOD IN THE
FOREGROUND
facing the CAMERA. The babel of the others comes in a
murmur over the scene.

GOD (quietly, without turning):
Yes, Gabriel.

GABRIEL'S VOICE:
Looks mighty nice, Lawd.

GOD:
Yes.

96. MED. CLOSE SHOT   GABRIEL AND OTHERS

GABRIEL (gazing down, the light still in his face):
Yes, suh. Dat'd make mighty nice farmin' country.

97. ANOTHER ANGLE   CLOSE SHOT OF GABRIEL FROM SIDE
The CAMERA catches a side view of Gabriel as he gazes down.

GABRIEL (still looking down):
Jes' look at dat south forty over dere.

He turns and starts to walk toward God, CAMERA TRUCK-
ING WITH HIM.[22]

GABRIEL (to God):
You ain't going to let dat go to waste, is you, Lawd?
Dat would be a pity an' a shame.

He stops beside God, the CAMERA STOPPING ALSO.

98. MED. CLOSE SHOT   GOD AND GABRIEL

GOD (not turning):
It's a good earth. Maybe I ought to have somebody
enjoy it. Gabriel, I'm goin' down dere.

GABRIEL:
Yes, Lawd.

GOD:
I want you to be my workin' boss yere while I'm
gone.

GABRIEL:
Yes, Lawd,

GOD:
Keep everythin' neat an' tidy.

GABRIEL:
Yes, Lawd.

GOD:

> You know dat sparrow dat fell a little while ago? 'Tend to dat, too.

GABRIEL:

> Yes, Lawd.

GOD:

> I guess dat's about all. (To assemblage.) Quiet, angels.

The murmuring of the assemblage stops.

99.   MED. CLOSE SHOT   GOD

GOD:

> I'm gonter pass one more miracle. You all gonter help me an' not make a soun' caize I'm gonter try— (thoughtfully) a new kind of a miracle. In my own image—(quietly) let dere be man.

There is a thunderclap and the choir begins to sing "In Bright Mansions Above," covering the following.

100.   MED. SHOT   GOD

slowly advancing up the incline toward the gates and away from the CAMERA through the hushed assemblage, which is lined up on either side. As he advances, the gates swing open toward the CAMERA. When God reaches opening the CAMERA approaches. God steps into space. From God's angle, we see:

101.   JACKMAN SHOT

The earth approaches the CAMERA at terrific speed. Streaks of light indicate stars, etc., approaching and passing God. As the earth comes so close that it is no longer a sphere but fills the screen, we can discern several unplowed fields with fences, a brook, and trees. Mist gathers, and we

DISSOLVE TO:

102. FULL SHOT   THE GARDEN OF EDEN
The garden is a heterogeneous cluster of cottonwood, camphor, live oak, and sycamore trees, yaupon and turkeyberry bushes, with their purple and red berries, sprays of fernlike indigo fiera, and splashes of various Louisiana flowers. As the mist rises and sunlight falls, Adam is disclosed in the center of the scene.

103. MED. SHOT   ADAM
He is a puzzled man of thirty, of medium height, dressed in the clothing of the average field hand, and bareheaded. He stands with his feet wide apart. Over the SHOT the choir continues "In Bright Mansions Above." Adam breathes consciously. Birds begin to sing.

104. CLOSE SHOT   ADAM
He hears the birds. Pleased and puzzled, he turns to look at the source of this novel sound. He senses his strength and raises his forearms, his fists clenched. With his left hand he carefully touches the muscles of his upper right arm. He smiles again, realizing his power. He looks at his feet and stamps once or twice, slowly realizing that he is an individual. Now there is a greater burst of birdsong, and, stretching out his arms, Adam glances at the foliage again, gives a deep sigh of satisfaction. The voices of the choir grow softer.

GOD'S VOICE (over the SHOT):
Good mo'nin', son.

Adam looks sharply off scene, a little awed.

ADAM:
Good mo'nin', Lawd.

105. MED. SHOT   GOD AND ADAM
God is now a natural man, and is treated as such by the CAMERA.

89

GOD:
What's yo' name, son?

ADAM:
Adam.

GOD:
Adam which?

ADAM (after a moment's puzzlement):
Jes' Adam, Lawd.

The choir stops.

106.   CLOSE SHOT   THE TWO
God crosses to Adam.

GOD (casually):
Well, Adam, how dey treatin' you? How things doin'?

ADAM:
Oh, I guess I'll make out all right as soon as I learn
de ropes.

GOD (inspecting Adam):
Yo' a nice job. Dey's one thing de matter wid you,
though. Adam, you need a family. Yes, sir, in yo'
heart you is a fam'ly man.

ADAM:
Yes suh. Lawd, what *is* a fam'ly?

GOD:
I'm gonter show you. Lay down dere, Adam. (Indi-
cating a spot.) Make out like you was goin' to
slumber.

ADAM:
Yes, Lawd.

107.   MED. SHOT   GOD AND ADAM
Adam lies down.

108.   CLOSE-UP   GOD
He smiles and murmurs softly:

GOD:
    Eve.

109.   CLOSE SHOT   ADAM AND EVE
exchanging glances, each awed by the other. Eve is young
and beautiful and dressed like a country girl, her gingham
dress new and clean.

GOD'S VOICE:
    Now you all right, Eve.

                                                PULL BACK TO:

110.   MED. SHOT   ADAM AND EVE
God is no longer to be seen. During the next three sen-
tences, Adam and Even look about them trying to see
God.

GOD'S VOICE:
    Now I'm gonter give you two de run of de whole
    garden.

111.   CLOSE SHOT   ADAM AND EVE

GOD'S VOICE:
    Jes' enjoy yo'selves. Drink de water from de little
    brooks an' de wine from de grapes an' de berries,
    an' eat de food dat's hangin' for you in de trees.

They look off scene right, smiling. There is a slight pause.

GOD'S VOICE:
    Dat is, in all but one tree.

Slowly their heads turn to the left and they gaze into the
air at something off scene. Their smiles disappear.

ADAM AND EVE (now gazing in terror off scene):
    Yes, Lawd.

112.   CLOSE-UP   ADAM
as he glances about anxiously to find God.

ADAM:
Thank you, Lawd.

113.   CLOSE-UP   EVE
She, too, looks about her.

EVE:
Thank you, Lawd.

114.   MED. SHOT   ADAM AND EVE

GOD'S VOICE:
I gotter be gittin' along now. I got a hund'ed thou-
san' things to do 'fo' you take yo' nex' breath. Enjoy
yo'selves—

115.   CLOSE SHOT   ADAM AND EVE
They look down and see that Adam's left hand and Eve's
right are clasped. Their heads raise slowly, and again they
look off scene left at the unseen tree.

116.   VERY CLOSE SHOT   ADAM AND EVE

EVE (in quiet terror):
Adam.

ADAM (also terrified):
What?

EVE (almost panic-stricken):
Adam.

The voices of the choir come over the following DISSOLVE,
singing "Don't Let Nobody Turn You 'Round."

DISSOLVE TO:

117.   FULL SHOT   FROM BELOW, OF THE HEAVENLY ASSEMBLAGE
peering over the embankment, into the CAMERA, as though

trying to warn Adam and Eve. The voices are now much louder. At the conclusion of the second verse,

FADE OUT[23]

FADE IN

118.   INT. SUNDAY SCHOOL   FULL SHOT   DAY
Mr. Deshee and the children are again present, but the groupings are slightly different. It is another Sunday.

DESHEE:
Now, I s'pose you chillun know what happened after God made Adam 'n' Eve. Do you?

MYRTLE (raising her hand):
I know, Mr. Deshee.

DESHEE (looking at Randolph):
Jes' a minute. Randolph!

119.   CLOSE SHOT   RANDOLPH
He is now playing on the floor beside Carlisle. He is eating an all-day sucker. His tongue is halted in making a stroke up the sucker. He looks at Mr. Deshee.

DESHEE'S VOICE:
Dis is de fifth time yo' sister ain't come wid you. Carlisle, take 'way dat truck he's eatin'. See kin you keep him quiet.

120.   CLOSE SHOT   CARLISLE AND RANDOLPH
Carlisle picks up Randolph and puts him on his lap.

121.   FULL SHOT   SUNDAY SCHOOL

DESHEE:
Now, den, Myrtle, what happened?

122.   CLOSE SHOT   MYRTLE

MYRTLE (smugly):
Why, den dey eat de fo'bidden fruit and den dey got driv' out de garden.

DESHEE'S VOICE:
An' den what happened?

MYRTLE (unprepared for another question):
Why, den dey felt ver' bad.

123.   CLOSE SHOT   MR. DESHEE

DESHEE:
I don' mean how dey feel, I mean how dey do. (Helpfully.) Do dey have any chillun or anything like dat?

124.   CLOSE-UP   MYRTLE

MYRTLE (enthusiastically):
Oh, yes. Why, dey have Cain 'n' Abel.

125.   MED. SHOT   SUNDAY SCHOOL

DESHEE:
Dat's right, an' one thing we know is dis boy Cain was a mean rascal on 'count caize he killed his brother.

DISSOLVE TO:

126.   MED. SHOT   CAIN   STANDING IN A PLOWED FIELD
At his feet lies the body of Abel. He holds a small rock in his right hand.

GOD'S VOICE (over SHOT):
Cain, look what you done to Abel.

127.   CLOSE-UP   CAIN
looking about frantically for the source of the voice.

CAIN:
Lawd, I was min'in' my own business. Wukkin' in de fiel'. He was sittin' in de shade of de tree. He say, "Me, I'd be skeered to git out in dis hot sun. I be 'fraid my brains git cooked. Co'se you ain't got no brains so you ain' in no danger." An' so I up an'

flang de rock. If I miss 'im all right—(his voice softens as he sees God off scene) if I hit 'im all right. Dat's de way I feel.

128. CLOSE SHOT GOD

GOD:
From now on dat's called a crime.

129. CLOSE SHOT CAIN

CAIN:
Well, what'd he want to come monkeyin' aroun' me fo' den? I was payin' him no min', and yere he come makin' me de fool. I'd bust anybody what make me de fool.

130. CLOSE SHOT GOD

GOD:
I say git yo'self down de road an' far away. An' you better git married an' settle down an' raise some chillun. Dey ain't nothin' to make a man fo'git his troubles like raisin' a fam'ly. Now, you better git.

131. MED. SHOT CAIN

CAIN:
Yessuh.

He looks at the rock, drops it, and walks off.

132. CLOSE-UP GOD
gazing after Cain. He shakes his head. The choir starts to sing "Run, Sinner, Run."

GOD:
Adam an' Eve you better try again. You better have Seth an' a lot mo' chillun.

DISSOLVE TO:

133.   EXT. BARREN COUNTRY ROAD   CLOSE SHOT   CAIN
WALKING

The choir is heard singing softly over scene. Cain continues walking until he comes to a leafy tree. Below it is an
old direction sign with the words:

LAND OF NOD
Parish Line

Cain and the CAMERA stop. The choir stops singing.

CAIN:

At las'! (He sits down on the stump of a tree, wiping
his forehead with a bandana.) Feels like I been
walkin' fo'ty years. (He takes out a cigarette and
scratches a match on his shoe.) Well, dey cain't git
me now. Now I kin raise a fam'ly.

An idea strikes him. He drops the match and the cigarette. He looks sharply to the right and left.

CAIN:

Well, I'll be bit by a mule! Where I gonter git dat
fam'ly? De Lawd went an' fooled me. Doggone!

134.   CLOSE SHOT   CAIN'S GIRL IN THE TREE
She is a blowzy, healthy country wench in her twenties.

CAIN'S GIRL:

Hello, Country Boy!

135.   CLOSE SHOT   CAIN   SHOOTING FROM THE TREE

CAIN (looking up):

Hey-ho, Good Lookin'! C'mon down 'ere.

136.   MED. SHOT   AT TREE   CAIN AND CAIN'S GIRL

CAIN'S GIRL:

I'm comin!

She drops to the ground and faces him.

CAIN'S GIRL:
> I bet you kin handle a gal mean wid dem big stout arms. I'd sho' hate to git you mad at me, Country Boy.

CAIN:
> Come yere. I ain' so mean.

She goes a little closer to him.

CAIN'S GIRL:
> I bet yo' hot coffee 'mongst de women folks.

CAIN (honestly enough):
> I ain' never find out. What was you doin' in dat tree?

CAIN'S GIRL:
> Jes' coolin' myself in de element.

CAIN:
> Is you a Nod Parish gal?

CAIN'S GIRL:
> Bo'n an' bred.

CAIN:
> You know, yo' kinda pretty.

CAIN'S GIRL:
> I bet you say dat to everybody all de way down de road.

137. CLOSE-UP   CAIN
He looks off scene, the conscious murderer.

CAIN:
> Comin' down dat road I didn't talk to nobody.

138. CLOSE SHOT   THE TWO

CAIN'S GIRL:
> Where you boun' for, Beautiful?

CAIN (nervously):
> I'm jes' seein' de country. Might settle down yere fo'
> a spell. Would yo' people like to take in a boarder?

CAIN'S GIRL:
> Be nice if dey would, wouldn't it?

CAIN:
> I think so. You got a beau?

CAIN'S GIRL:
> Huh-uh!

CAIN:
> You has now.

CAIN'S GIRL:
> Think you kin walk a little further now, City Boy?

CAIN:
> Yeh, I ain't so weary now.

He picks up his bundle. She takes his arm.

CAIN'S GIRL:
> What's yo' name?

CAIN:
> Cain.

CAIN'S GIRL (vaguely disturbed, but accepting her doom):
> Den I'm Cain's gal. (She tries to be gay.) Come on,
> honey, an' meet de folks.

CAMERA FOLLOWS them as they start to walk away.[24]

139.   CLOSE SHOT   GOD
standing nearby, watching off scene.

GOD (shaking his head):
> Bad business. I don't like de way things is goin' atall.

Cloud effects (JACKMAN) cover the following

FADE OUT

FADE IN

140.   INT. GOD'S PRIVATE OFFICE   CLOSE-UP   GABRIEL

GABRIEL:
Well, I guess dat's about all de impo'tant business dis mo'nin', Lawd.

PULL BACK TO:

141.   MED. SHOT   OFFICE
It is a small room. A large window looks out on the sky. There is a battered rolltop desk. On the wall next to the window is a framed religious oleograph. A door is at the left. In the corner to right of window is a small old-fashioned safe. A hat rack is on the wall above the door. There are two or three cheap pine chairs beside the window, and beyond the door. Facing the desk, God is seated in an old swivel armchair that creaks every time God leans back in it. The desk is open and various papers are stuck in the pigeonholes. Writing implements, etc., are on the desk. On a shelf above the desk is a row of law books. A cuspidor is near the desk, and a wastebasket by it. The general atmosphere is that of the office of a Negro lawyer in a Louisiana town. Gabriel is sitting in one of the chairs with a pencil in hand, a notebook on his lap. He is checking off items in the notebook with his pencil. He turns back one page and looks up.[25]

142.   CLOSE SHOT   GOD
working at the desk, his back toward the CAMERA.

GOD:
How 'bout dat cherub over to archangel Montgomery's house?

143.   CLOSE SHOT   GABRIEL

GABRIEL:
Where do dey live, Lawd?

GOD'S VOICE:
> Dat little two-story gold house, over by de pearly
> gates.

GABRIEL (suddenly remembering):
> Oh, *dat* Montgomery. I thought you was referrin' to
> de ol' gentleman. Oh, yeh. (He sorts through the
> items and finds one he is looking for.) Yere 'tis. (He
> reads awkwardly.) "Cherub Christina Montgomery;
> wings is moltin' out of season an' nobody know what
> to do."

144.   MED. CLOSE SHOT   THE TWO

GOD (his back still to Gabriel):
> Well, now, take keer of dat. You gotter be more care-
> ful, Gabe.

GABRIEL:
> Yes, Lawd.

He carefully closes the notebook as God goes to work on
some papers at his desk. Gabriel cracks his knuckles and
drums with his fingers on his lap. He looks down and
sees something beside his chair.

145.   CLOSE SHOT   GABRIEL
picking up a horn. He looks at it and breathes a sigh of
pleased anticipation. He sees a spot on its highly polished
surface and instantly removes it with the cloth of his robe.
He wets his lips and purses them as if to blow on the
horn and slowly brings the mouthpiece to his mouth.

146.   MED. SHOT   GOD AND GABRIEL

GOD (quietly, as he puts a document in a pigeonhole):
> Now, watch yo'self, Gabriel.

Gabriel looks at God, startled.

147. CLOSE-UP   GABRIEL

GABRIEL:
> I wasn't goin' to blow, Lawd. I jes' do dat every now
> an' den so I kin keep de feel of it.

148. MED SHOT   GOD AND GABRIEL
God picks up the last remaining paper on his desk and
looks at it.

GOD:
> What's dis yere about de moon?

149. CLOSE SHOT   GABRIEL

GABRIEL:
> Oh! De moon people say it's beginnin' to melt a little,
> on 'count caize de sun's so hot.

150. CLOSE SHOT   GOD

GOD:
> It's goin' 'roun' 'cordin' to schedule, ain't it?

GABRIEL'S VOICE:
> Yes, Lawd.

GOD:
> Well, dere's nothin' de matter wid dat moon. Trouble
> is so many angels go flyin' over dere on Saddy night.
> Dey git to beatin' dere wings when dey dancin' an'
> dat makes de heat. (He swings slowly in his chair.)
> Tell dem from now on dancin' 'roun' de moon is sin-
> nin'. Dey got to stop it. Dat'll cool off de moon.

He swings back comfortably in his chair; he clasps his
hands behind his head.

GOD:
> Anythin' else you ought to remin' me of?

151.   MED. SHOT   GOD AND GABRIEL

GABRIEL:
De prayers, Lawd.

GOD (puzzled):
De prayers? (Starting to unclasp his hands.)

GABRIEL:
From mankind. You know, down on de earth.

GOD (swinging his chair around, facing Gabriel):
Oh, yeh, de poor little earth. Bless my soul, I almos'
forgot about dat.

He rises and goes to the window and looks down.

GOD:
Mus' be three or four hund'ed years since I been
down dere.

152.   LONG SHOT   THE EARTH   SEEN FROM GOD'S
WINDOW   (JACKMAN)
The earth now has little houses on it, roads, a couple of
churches, etc.

GOD'S VOICE (over SHOT):
I wasn't any too pleased wid dat job.

153.   MED. SHOT   GOD'S OFFICE   GABRIEL IN THE FOREGROUND
God still looks out of the window.

GABRIEL (laughing as he hangs up his horn on a wall
peg):
You know you don' make no mistakes, Lawd.

154.   CLOSE SHOT   GOD

GOD (slowly):
So dey tell me. I fin' I kin be displeased though, an'
I *was* displeased wid de mankind I las' seen. (He
turns musingly from the window.) Maybe I ought to
go down dere ag'in—I need a little holiday.

155. MED. SHOT   GOD AND GABRIEL

GABRIEL:
   Might do you good, Lawd.

GOD:
   I guess I will. (Crossing toward the door.) I'll go an'
   see how dem poor humans is makin' out. What time
   is it, by de sun an' de stars?

Gabriel goes to the window.

156. CLOSE SHOT   GABRIEL, FACING THE CAMERA
He glances out the window, making a half-arc with his
head.

GABRIEL:
   Jes' exactly half past, Lawd.

157. MED. SHOT   GOD IN FOREGROUND NEAR DOOR
He is taking his hat and stick from the hat rack. Gabriel
turns toward the Lord.

GOD:
   Well, take keer o' yo'self. I'll be back Saddy.

He starts out. The voices of the choir come over as the
DISSOLVE starts. They are singing "Dere's No Hidin' Place
Down Dere." The singing continues over the following
cloud effect and

DISSOLVE TO:

158. LONG SHOT   FROM BELOW   OF THE CHOIR LEANING OVER
THE EDGE OF HEAVEN   (PROCESS)
Again they are looking down toward the CAMERA from
the embankment, as they sing.

159. EXT. COUNTRY ROAD   TRUCK SHOT   GOD WALKING   DAY
The road is an idyllic version of the same road Mr. Deshee
walked on the way to Sunday school, only there are more
trees. The singing of the choir decreases in volume and
distant church bells catch God's attention.

160.　LONG SHOT　A DISTANT VILLAGE
A church is conspicuous. The choir and the church bells stop.

CUT BACK TO:

161.　CLOSE SHOT　GOD

GOD:
Dat's nice. Nice and quiet. Dat's de way I like Sunday to be.

162.　CLOSE TRUCK SHOT　GOD
The CAMERA TRUCKS before God, as he resumes his walk. The sound of a ukulele and Zeba's voice singing a whining blues is heard. God looks off scene a little to the left.

163.　CLOSE SHOT　ZEBA
sitting on a tree stump, playing a ukulele. She is a flashily dressed wanton of about eighteen. The CAMERA IS MOVING toward her as God approaches.

164.　CLOSE SHOT　GOD　CAMERA STILL TRUCKING BEFORE HIM

GOD:
Now, dat ain't so good.

165.　MED. SHOT　GOD AND ZEBA　THE CAMERA HAS STOPPED
God stands beside her.

GOD:
Stop dat!

ZEBA:
What's de matter wid you, Country Boy? Pull up yo' pants. (She resumes singing.)

166.　CLOSE SHOT　GOD

GOD (quietly):
Stop dat.

167.   CLOSE SHOT   ZEBA, FROM ABOVE   GOD'S ANGLE

ZEBA:

Listen to me, Banjo Eyes. What right you got to stop a lady enjoyin' herself?

GOD'S VOICE:

Dis is de Sabbath. Dat's no kin' o' song to sing on de Lawd's day.

ZEBA:

Who care 'bout de Lawd's day, anymo'? People jes' use Sunday now to git over Saddy.

168.   CLOSE SHOT   THE TWO

GOD:

You a awful sassy little girl.

ZEBA:

I come fum sassy people! We even speak mean of de dead.

GOD:

What's yo' name?

ZEBA:

"What's my name?" Ain't you de ol'-time gal hunter! Fust, "What's my name?" den I s'pose, what would it be like if you tried to kiss me? You preachers is de debbil.

GOD (gently):

I ain't aimin' to tetch you, daughter.

169.   CLOSE SHOT   ZEBA   FROM GOD'S ANGLE

She looks at God. His voice now has the rumble of thunder but is not loud.

GOD'S VOICE:

What is yo' name?

ZEBA:
> Zeba.

GOD'S VOICE:
> Who's yo' fam'ly?

ZEBA:
> I'm de great-great-gran'daughter of Seth.

170. CLOSE SHOT   GOD

GOD:
> Of Seth? Seth was a good man.

171. CLOSE SHOT   THE TWO

ZEBA:
> Yeh, he too good, he die of holiness.

GOD:
> An' yere's his little gran'daughter reekin' wid co-
> logne. Ain't nobody ever tol' you yo' on de road to
> hell?

ZEBA (at ease again):
> Sho' dat's what de preacher say. Exceptin' of course
> I happens to know dat I'm on de road to de picnic
> grounds, an' at de present time I'm waitin' to keep a
> engagement wid my sweet papa. (She becomes
> slightly sinister.) He don' like people talkin' to me.
> (She looks off scene, calling.) Hello, sugah!

172. LONG SHOT   CAIN THE SIXTH   FROM THE ANGLE OF ZEBA
AND GOD
He is approaching up the road. He is a young buck, wearing a "box" coat and the other flashy garments of a Ram-
part Street swell.

CAIN THE SIXTH (calling):
> Hi, mama! (Nearer.) Sorry I'm late, baby, but de gals
> in de barrelhouse jes' wouldn't let me go. Doggone,
> one little wirehead swore she'd tear me down.

173.   MED. SHOT   THE GROUP
Cain the Sixth steps between God and Zeba, to share the tree stump.

GOD:
    What's yo' name, son?

CAIN THE SIXTH (contemptuously, without turning):
    Soap 'n' water, Country Boy.

174.   CLOSE SHOT   CAIN THE SIXTH AND ZEBA
Cain is suddenly frightened by an unseen cause.

GOD'S VOICE (again with the depth of thunder):
    What is yo' name, son?

CAIN THE SIXTH:
    Cain the Sixth.

175.   CLOSE SHOT   GOD

GOD (musingly):
    I was afraid so.

176.   CLOSE SHOT   CAIN THE SIXTH
He is looking straight ahead, still paralyzed, but his fear leaves him, and he slowly turns around to look up at God. As he sees him, his fears leave.

CAIN THE SIXTH:
    You—you a new preacher?

177.   MED. SHOT.   GROUP

GOD:
    Where you live?

CAIN THE SIXTH:
    Me? I live mos' any place.

GOD:
    Yes, an' you gonter see dem all. Is de udder young men all like you?

107

CAIN THE SIXTH (smilingly, turning to Zeba):
De gals don' think so.

Zeba sits on his lap.

ZEBA:
Dey ain't nobody in de worl' like my honeycake.

She starts to play. Cain the Sixth stops her.

178.   CLOSE SHOT   ZEBA AND CAIN THE SIXTH

CAIN THE SIXTH (with acid sweetness):
Dey tell me las' night you was talkin' to a creeper man, baby.

ZEBA (innocently):
Why, you know dey ain't nobody in de worl' fo' me but you.

CAIN THE SIXTH:
I know dey ain't. I even got dat guaranteed. (He takes a revolver from his pocket.) See dat, honey?

ZEBA:
Uh-huh.

CAIN THE SIXTH:
Dat jes' makes me positive. (He puts the gun back.)

ZEBA:
You don' wanter believe dem stories, papa.

CAIN THE SIXTH (with sinister lightness):
Oh, I didn't believe dem. Co'se dat big gorilla, Flatfoot, from de udder side of de river *is* in town ag'in.

ZEBA:
Why, Flatfoot ain't nothin' to me.

CAIN THE SIXTH:
Co'se he ain't. Go 'head, sing some mo', baby.

Zeba resumes singing.[26]

179. CLOSE SHOT   GOD

GOD:
    Bad business.

He resumes his walking, the CAMERA TRUCKING with him.
There is a twitter of birds. God looks up.

180. CLOSE SHOT   BIRDS ON A BRANCH
They are preening themselves and singing.

181. CLOSE SHOT   GOD   CAMERA TRUCKING WITH HIM

GOD:
    De birds goin' 'bout dere business, all right.

He looks down.

GOD:
    How you little flowers makin' out?

182. CLOSE SHOT   SOME FLOWERS, MOSTLY DAISIES
Their heads lift as if by a breeze.

CHILDREN'S VOICES (over SHOT):
    We okay, Lawd.

183. CLOSE SHOT   GOD

GOD:
    Yes, an' you look mighty pretty.

184. CLOSE SHOT   FLOWERS

CHILDREN'S VOICES:
    Thank you, Lawd.

185. CLOSE SHOT   GOD WALKING   CAMERA AGAIN TRUCKING
BESIDE HIM

GOD:
    It's only de human bein's makes me downhearted.
    Yere's as nice a Sunday as dey is turnin' out any-

where, an' nobody makin' de right use of it. (He looks off scene.) Now dat's nice to see people prayin'. I thought dey did it in church. But I fin' I don' min' if dey do it outdoors.

186. LONG SHOT   BY THE SIDE OF THE ROAD, A GROUP OF FIVE ADULT NEGROES AND A BOY
on their knees in a semicircle. The CAMERA TRUCKS TOWARD THEM FROM GOD'S ANGLE. At the beginning of the SHOT they appear to be praying.

BOY:
Oh, Lawd, de smokehouse is empty. Oh, Lawd, lemme git dem groceries. Oh, Lawd, lemme see dat little *six*. (He casts the dice.) Wham!

187. CLOSE-UP   THE DICE ON THE GROUND
A two and a four.

BOY'S VOICE:
Dere she is, frien's.

188. MED. SHOT   GROUP
as God approaches.

AD LIB EXCLAMATIONS:
Well, bus' down my door! Doggone, dat's de eighth pass he make! He's de debbil's baby today, all right!

The boy is picking up the money.

189. CLOSE-UP   GOD
looking over the group's shoulders.

GOD:
Gamblin'! (He looks down.) An' wid frozen dice!

190. CLOSE-UP   BOY GAMBLER

BOY:
Dey's a dolla' 'n' a half talkin' fo' me. How much you want, Riney?

191.   CLOSE-UP   FIRST GAMBLER
who is secretly counting some money in his hand.

FIRST GAMBLER:
I take fo' bits. Wait a minute. Mebbe I take a little mo'.

192.   CLOSE SHOT   SECOND GAMBLER
glancing up at God.

SECOND GAMBLER:
Hello, Liver Lips. (To the others.) Lookit ol' Liver Lips.

193.   MED. SHOT   GROUP
The others look up, laughing good-naturedly. One or two repeat the phrase "Liver Lips."

FIRST GAMBLER:
Ain't his pockets high from de groun'? Ol' High Pockets!

194.   CLOSE-UP   BOY GAMBLER
looking at first gambler.

BOY:
Come on, you gonter fade me or not?

God's hand comes down and seizes the boy's ear. Astonishment comes over his face as he is pulled up from the ground.

195.   CLOSE SHOT   GOD AND THE BOY

GOD:
Why, yo' jes' a little boy. Gamblin' an' sinnin', an' chewin' tobacco, like you was yo' daddy. (He sniffs.) You been drinkin' sonny-kick-mammy-wine, too. (He turns to the others.) An' you gamblers oughta be 'shamed, leadin' dis boy to sin.

111

196.   CLOSE SHOT   FIRST GAMBLER
with an outraged innocence:

FIRST GAMBLER:
   Why, he de bes' crap shooter in town, mister.

197.   CLOSE SHOT   GOD

GOD:
   Mebbe I oughta tell his mammy. I bet she don' know
   'bout dis.

198.   CLOSE SHOT   FIRST GAMBLER:

FIRST GAMBLER:
   See kin you beat 'im, High Pockets. Dey's a dolla'
   open yere.

199.   MED SHOT   GROUP

GOD:
   I ain't gonter beat 'im. I mus' teach 'im. I may have
   to teach you all.

God walks out of the SHOT. We STAY ON GROUP. Their
eyes follow him off scene for a moment.

BOY:
   If you kin fin' my mammy you do mo'n I kin.

200.   CLOSE SHOT   FIRST GAMBLER

FIRST GAMBLER:
   His mammy run off las' week wid a railroad man.
   She's *e*-loped.

201.   MED. SHOT   GROUP OF GAMBLERS

BOY:
   Who wants any part of de dolla'?

The others resume their interest in the game.

AD LIB EXCLAMATIONS:
    Oh, I'll take anoder two bits. Gimme a dime's wo'th.
I ain't only got fifteen cents lef'.[27]

                          DISSOLVE TO:

202.   MED SHOT   GOD
    walking through a small village. CAMERA TRUCKS before
him. The sound of music from pianos in different parts,
played disjointedly, and the scattered laughter of men's
and women's voices is heard. God looks down.

203.   CLOSE SHOT   GOD
    observing the empty whiskey bottle at his feet. He looks
up.

204.   MED. SHOT   BALCONY OF ONE OF THE HOUSES
    On the balcony a drunk is dancing with an unkempt girl.
Another man is seated with a drunken girl on his lap.
Both are almost asleep, so the pictorial relationship is that
of an old-time ventriloquist and his dummy. Seated on
the floor of the balcony and peering through the railings
is another drunken girl, yelling "woo" to passersby. Another man is standing beside the girl. He is finishing a
bottle which she takes from his lips. She tries to get
something from it and notices that it is empty. She pitches
it into the street.

205.   MED. CLOSE SHOT   GOD
    looking at the second bottle which is lying near the first.
He resumes his walk out of CAMERA.

                        QUICK DISSOLVE:

206.   MED. SHOT   GOD
    as he walks into group of two men, one of whom is sitting
at the base of a streetlamp. He is drunk. Leaning against
the lamp is another man, who is watching a third man
unhitching a mule from an old surrey, in which the oc-
cupant is asleep, the reins held loosely in his hand.

207.   MED. CLOSE SHOT   MAN
leaning against pole.

208.   TWO SHOT   MAN AGAINST POLE AND MAN UNHITCHING
MULE

MAN AGAINST POLE:
Wha' you gonna do wid him?

MAN WITH MULE:
I gonna sell 'im.

MAN AGAINST POLE:
What if dat man dat owns him wakes up?

209.   CLOSE SHOT   MAN SLEEPING IN SURREY

VOICE OF MAN WITH MULE:
He won't wake up.

210.   TWO SHOT

MAN AT POLE (as the man continues unhitching mule):
Doggone—you is quite a boy!

211.   CLOSE SHOT   GOD
shaking his head.

QUICK DISSOLVE TO:

212.   EXT. DILAPIDATED CABIN
with dispossessed notice beside door. Three little children are crying beside a flashily dressed but hapless Ne-
gress in foreground. Two tough-looking men are carrying
out the possessions through the door, under the supervision of a third man.

213.   MED. SHOT   GOD
stopping and watching the proceedings.

214.   GROUP IN FRONT OF CABIN
The men dump chairs and bedding on the ground.

DISPOSSESSED WOMAN (to man in charge):
　You expect us to sleep on de groun'?

MAN IN CHARGE:
　I don't cah' where you sleep. See you clear dat stuff
　away.

Behind him one of the helpers closes and locks the door
of the cabin. The man in charge walks away with the
other two, as God walks into the SHOT to sympathize with
the woman. Her back is toward God. The kids now stick
their tongues out at the departing dispossessors.

215.　MED. CLOSE SHOT　MOTHER AND CHILDREN
　God in background, watching.

DISPOSSESSED WOMAN (taking money from her blouse):
　Wait'll he gits aroun' de corner befo' we put de things
　back.

OLDEST CHILD:
　We's all out of gin.

DISPOSSESSED WOMAN (opening purse):
　Well, you better go buy some.

As she is taking out the money she addresses the other
two.

DISPOSSESSED WOMAN:
　Now what you two gonna do dis afternoon?

SECOND CHILD:
　I'se gonna rob a grocery store.

THIRD CHILD:
　An' I'se gonna pick pockets.

DISPOSSESSED WOMAN (handing first child money):
　Dat's right—dat's right. Don't git arrested.[28]

216.   CLOSE SHOT   GOD

He is horrified at what he has seen. He goes on walking,
CAMERA TRUCKING before him.

QUICK DISSOLVE TO:

217.   MED SHOT   GOD WALKING

again, CAMERA TRUCKING before him. Noah walks into
the scene behind God, approaches, and is abreast of him.
Noah is a thin, elderly preacher. His coat is of the ham-
mer-tail variety. He carries a prayer book under his arm.

NOAH:

Mo'nin', brother.

GOD:

Mo'nin'. (Puzzled for a moment.) I declah you look
like a good man.

NOAH:

I try to be. I'm de preacher yere. (A little critically.) I
don't think I seen you to de meetin'.

GOD:

I jes' come to town a little while ago. I been pretty
busy.

NOAH:

Mos' everybody *say* dey pretty busy. So busy dey
cain't come to meetin'. Seem like de mo' I preaches,
de mo' people ain't got time to come to church. Today dey wasn't even members fo' de choir. I had to
do de preachin' an' de bassin' too.

GOD:

Is dat a fac'?

NOAH:

Um-hm. Everybody is *mighty* busy, gamblin', good-
timin', an' goin' on.

GOD:

Seems a pity. Dey all perfec'ly healthy?

116

NOAH:

> Oh, dey healthy, all right. Dey jes' all lazy, an' mean, an' full of sin. You look like a preacher, too, brother.

218. CLOSE-UP   GOD

GOD:

> I am, in a way.

219. CLOSE SHOT   THE TWO   WALKING, CAMERA TRUCKING WITH THEM

NOAH:

> You jes' passin' through de neighborhood?

GOD:

> Jes' lookin' it ovah. It's enough to discourage you.

NOAH:

> Oh, I gotta keep wras'lin' wid 'em. Where you bound fo' right now, brother?

GOD:

> I'm about ready to go back.

NOAH:

> Uh-huh. Well, I live right yere.

220. MED SHOT   A CLEAN LITTLE CABIN
God and Noah, and the CAMERA, stop.

NOAH:

> Why don' you stop an' give us de pleasure of yo' comp'ny fo' dinner? I believe my ol' woman has kilt a chicken.

GOD:

> Why, dat's mighty nice of you, brother—I don' believe I caught yo' name.

221.   CLOSE SHOT   THE TWO

NOAH:

Noah, jes' Noah. Dis is my home, brother. Come right in.

They start through the little yard in front of the cabin. The choir begins to sing "You Gonna Sit Down at de Welcome Table," covering the

DISSOLVE TO:

222.   INT. NOAH'S HOUSE   MED. SHOT

It is a simple cabin interior, with neat, clean curtains over the windows, a framed picture of "Jerusalem the Golden," and a "God Bless Our Home" sign. At the beginning of the scene, we see Noah leading God into the room. Mrs. Noah, a pleasant-faced woman of sixty, enters the scene. She wipes her hands on a neat apron as she advances, and in pantomime is introduced to God. The music of the choir continues softly over the following dialogue.

NOAH (as Mrs. Noah takes the men's hats):

Dis gemman's a preacher, too, darlin'. He's passin' through de country.

MRS. NOAH:

Oh, dat's fine. You jes' ketch me when I'm gittin' dinner ready. Sit right down yere. (She indicates the table.) I got a chicken in de pot an' it'll be ready in 'bout five minutes.

223.   CLOSE SHOT

as the men seat themselves at the table, Mrs. Noah behind them.

MRS. NOAH (to Noah):

I'll go out de back an' call Shem, Ham, 'n' Japheth. (To God.) Dey's our sons. Dey live right acrost de way but always have Sunday dinner wid us. You mens make yo'selves comf'table.

GOD:
Thank you, thank you very kindly.

NOAH:
You run along, we all right.

The music stops, as Mrs. Noah leaves the scene.

224.   CLOSE TWO SHOT   GOD AND NOAH

GOD:
You got a fine wife, Brother Noah.

NOAH (complacently):
She a pretty good woman.

GOD (musingly, looking about him):
Yes, suh, an' a nice little home. Have a ten-cent seegar?

He produces the cigar.

NOAH (delighted):
Thank you, much obliged.

GOD (as Noah lights his cigar):
Jes' what seems to be de main trouble 'mong mankind, Noah?

225.   CLOSE SHOT   NOAH

NOAH:
Well, it seems to me de main trouble is dat de whol' distric' is wide open. Dat makes fo' loose livin'. Men folks spen' all de time fightin', loafin' an' gamblin', an' makin' bad likker.

226.   CLOSE SHOT   GOD

GOD:
What about de women?

227. CLOSE TWO SHOT

NOAH:

De women is worse dan de men. If dey ain't makin'
love powder dey out beg, borrow, an' stealin' money
fo' policy tickets. Doggone, I come in de church Sunday 'fo' las' 'bout an' hour befo' de meetin' was to
start, an' dere was a lady stealin' de altar cloth. She
was goin' to hock it. Dey ain't got no moral sense.

GOD:

Terrible, terrible.

NOAH:

Yes, suh. Dis use' to be a nice, decent community.
But now it seems like every time I preach de Word
de place goes a little mo' to de dogs. De good Lawd
only knows what's gonter happen.[29]

228. CLOSE-UP GOD

GOD (softly):

Dat is de truth.

229. CLOSE TWO SHOT

Noah sighs over the sadness of things, takes a puff of his
cigar, and suddenly reaches down and clasps his knee
and twists his foot.

NOAH:

Hmm!

GOD (not looking at him):

What's de matter?

NOAH:

I jes' got a twitch. My buck ague, I guess, Every now
an' den I gets a twitch in de knee. Might be a sign of
rain.

GOD:

> Dat's jes' what it is. Noah, what's de mos' rain you ever had 'roun' dese parts?

NOAH:

> Well, de water come down fo' six days steady las' April an' de ribber got so swole it bus' down de levee up 'bove Freeport. Raise cain all de way down to de delta.

GOD:

> What would you say was it to rain fo' fo'ty days an' fo'ty nights?

NOAH:

> I'd say dat was a *complete* rain!

GOD:

> Noah, you don't know who I is, do you?

230.   CLOSE-UP   NOAH

NOAH (puzzled):

> Yo' face looks easy, but I don't think I recall de name.

STAY on Noah as a light roll of thunder is heard and the light on Noah's face increases. His mouth opens in awe, as the light grows stronger, and his eyes lift as though he were looking at something several feet above his head. Slowly the light fades and Noah lowers his eyes until, simultaneous with the return to the lighting of the previous scene, he is again looking directly across the table at God.

231.   MED. SHOT   GOD AND NOAH

Noah rises, his hands clasped, head bent in humility.

NOAH:

> I should have known you. I should have seen de glory.

GOD (not looking at him):

Dat's all right, Noah. You didn't know who I was.

NOAH:

I'm jes' ol' preacher Noah, Lawd, an' I'm yo' servant. I ain't very much, but I'se all I got.

GOD:

Sit down, Noah. Don't let me hear you shamin' yo'self, caize yo' a good man (Noah timidly seats himself) far as I kin see, you an' yo' fam'ly is de only respectable people in de worl'.

NOAH:

Dey jes' all poor sinners, Lawd.

232.   CLOSE-UP   GOD

GOD:

I know. I am yo' Lawd. I am a god of wrath an vengeance an' dat's why I'm gonter destroy dis worl'.[30]

233.   CLOSE-UP   NOAH

NOAH:

Jes' as you say, Lawd.

234.   MED. SHOT   GOD AND NOAH

GOD (taking a pencil and a piece of paper from his pocket):

Noah, I want you to build me a boat. I want you to call it de—(he looks up to find the word) de "ark," an' I want it to look like dis. (He continues drawing on the paper.)

235.   CLOSE SHOT   GOD

The choir softly begins singing "I Want To Be Ready."

GOD:

I want you to take two of every kind of animal an' bird dat's in de country. I want you to take seeds an' sprouts an' everythin' like dat an' put dem on dat ark, becaize dere is gonter be all dat rain. Dey's gonter be a deluge, Noah, an' dey's gonter be a flood. De levees is gonter bus' an' everythin' dat's fastened down is comin' loose, but it ain't gonter float long— (his voice increases in volume to the end of the speech) caize I'm gonter make a storm dat'll sink everythin' from a hen coop to a barn. Dey ain't a ship on de sea dat'll be able to fight dat tempest. Dey all got to go. Everythin'. Everythin' in dis pretty worl' I made.

236.   MED. SHOT   GOD AND NOAH
There is a slight pause. God's voice drops.

GOD:

Except one thing, Noah, You an' yo' fam'ly an' de things I said are gonter ride dat storm in de ark. Yere's de way it's to be.

He hands Noah the paper. The singing stops. (NOTE: Under no conditions should the details on the paper be picked up by the CAMERA.)

NOAH (looking at paper):

Yes, suh, dis seems to be complete. (He looks up.) Now, 'bout the animals. You say you want everythin'?

GOD:

Two of everythin'.

NOAH:

Dat would include jayraffes an' hippopotamuses?

GOD:

Everythin' dat is.

NOAH:

Dey was a circus in town. I guess I kin fin' dem. Co'se I kin git all de rabbits an' possums an' wil' turkeys easy. I'll sen' de boys out. (A new idea possesses him.) Hmm, I'm jes' wonderin'—

GOD:
'Bout what?

NOAH:
'Bout snakes. Think you'd like snakes, too?

GOD:
Certainly, I want snakes.

NOAH:
Oh, I kin git snakes, lots of 'em. (A little too casually.) Co'se, some of 'em's a little dangerous. Maybe I better take a kag of likker, too?

GOD:
You kin have a kag of likker.

NOAH:
Yes, suh, dey's a awful lot of differ'nt kin's of snakes, come to think about it. Dey's water moccasins, cotton moufs, rattlers—mus' be a hund'ed kin's of other snakes down in de swamps. Maybe I better take two kags of likker.

GOD:
I think de one kag's enough.

NOAH:
No, I better take two kags. Besides, I kin put one on each side of de boat, an' balance de ship wid dem as well as havin' dem fo' medicinal use.

GOD:
You kin put one kag in de middle of de ship.

237. CLOSE SHOT   NOAH

NOAH:
Jes' as easy to take de two kags, Lawd.

GOD'S VOICE:
I think one kag's enough.

NOAH:

Yes, Lawd, but you see, fo'ty days and fo'ty nights—

There is a light roll of thunder and a suggestion of the extra illumination on Noah's face.

GOD'S VOICE:

One kag, Noah.

NOAH:

Yes, Lawd, one kag.

The light fades on his face. (The choir resumes singing "I Want To Be Ready," covering the following DISSOLVE.)

DISSOLVE TO:

238–40. OMITTED.[31]

241.   MED. LONG SHOT   THE ARK

is seen in the distance. THE CAMERA IS ON A BOOM and MOVES UP to a CLOSE-UP of Noah, who is seated on a high stool at an old-fashioned clerk's desk, which is near the top of the gangplank. He has a sheet of paper perhaps twelve feet long, the top of which is on the desk, the rest trailing over onto the deck. (While the CAMERA remained in the LONG SHOT we SHOW three boys working around the ark.)

NOAH (calling):

Shem! Ham! Japheth! Come yere a minute!

The three boys approach.

242.   CLOSE SHOT   NOAH

He is wearing a captain's uniform, a slicker and a silk hat. He is smoking a pipe. He looks up.

NOAH:

I'se been checkin' de livestock ag'in.

The three boys enter the SHOT.

NOAH:
Dey's one thing missin' in de *A*'s.

243.   CLOSE-UP   LIST
written in an unskilled hand. At the top are the names:
2 Alligators
2 Angleworms
2 Aardvarks
2 Alley cats
2 Archipeligos
2 Ants
2 American eagles

NOAH'S VOICE (OVER SHOT):
What'd you fin' out about dis one?

His finger points to:
Aardvarks

[244–45.]   CLOSE SHOT   GROUP
Ham is looking over Noah's shoulder.

HAM:
Oh! De circus people say dey don't have any.

NOAH:
I guess we'll have to order dem through de Lawd,
too.

Noah lifts part of the sheet of paper and half-audibly
checks over other items.

NOAH:
" . . . buffaloes, bedbugs, butterflies . . . " I guess de
B's is all right.

Ham looks up startled.

HAM (yelling):
Bees!

He dashes off.

NOAH:
> Dat's right. (He writes.)

246.   CLOSE-UP LIST
> We see Noah's handwriting:
>> 2 Bees

247.   CLOSE SHOT NOAH AND JAPHETH

JAPHETH:
> Pretty near suppertime, Daddy.

NOAH:
> Maybe so, but I got de feelin' we all gotta keep goin'.

FIRST WOMAN'S VOICE (over SHOT):
> You gonter work all night, Noah, maybe, huh?

NOAH:
> If de sperrit move me.
>> CUT TO:

248.   MED. SHOT FROM NOAH'S ANGLE A FLASHILY DRESSED WOMAN
who is one of a group of four who are watching the proceedings from the ground. The others include a flashily dressed widow, a tall, evil-looking man, and a little girl who has a contemptuous sneer on her face. Several shocks of corn as high as humans are to be seen.

FIRST WOMAN:
> Look yere, Noah, whyn't you give up all dis foolishness? Don' you know people sayin' yo' crazy? What you think you doin' anyway?

249.   CLOSE SHOT NOAH

NOAH:
> I'se buildin' a ark. (He consults his list again.) " . . . foxes, fireflies, an' fleas."

127

250.   MED. SHOT   ANOTHER GROUP OF VILLAGERS
including two highly painted schoolgirls, laughing and
pointing.

FIRST SCHOOLGIRL (pointing off scene):
    Look, dey won't be able to pay off de grocery store
    fo' ten years!

251.   MED. SHOT   AT GANGPLANK   OF MRS. NOAH AND THE
WIVES OF SHEM, HAM, AND JAPHETH
Mrs. Noah is pushing a wheelbarrow loaded down with
groceries, hams, loaves of bread, etc. Following her are
Ham's and Shem's wives, also loaded down with bundles.
Japheth's wife is carrying a kitchen stove. They are all
going up the gangplank.

252.   MED. SHOT   ANOTHER GROUP ON THE GROUND

SECOND WOMAN (calling):
    Noah, do you know yo' ol' lady is tellin' everybody
    it's gonter rain fo' fo'ty days an' fo'ty nights?

253.   MED. SHOT   MRS. NOAH AND HER DAUGHTERS-IN-LAW
continuing up the gangplank. Their heads raise proudly
in disdain.

NOAH'S VOICE:
    Lot I keer what you think.

254.   CLOSE SHOT   ZEBA AND FLATFOOT
Flatfoot is a tall, black, wicked-looking buck. They are
looking up at the ark, their arms around each other's
waists.

ZEBA:
    Dere it is, baby. Was I lyin'?

FLATFOOT:
    Well, I'll be split in two!

255. MED. SHOT   TAKING IN OTHER ONLOOKERS

MAN:
> What do you think of it, Flatfoot?

FLATFOOT:
> I mus' say! Look to me like a house wit' a warpin' cellar.

256. CLOSE SHOT   NOAH
looking up.

NOAH:
> Dis yere vessel is a boat.

257. CLOSE SHOT   FLATFOOT

FLATFOOT:
> When I was a little boy dey used to build boats down near de ribber, where de water was.

257A. THE CROWD
laughing, including Flatfoot.

258. CLOSE SHOT   NOAH

NOAH:
> Dis time it's been arranged to have de water come up to de boat.

259–60. OMITTED

261. TWO GAMBLERS
followed by Cain the Sixth, enter the SHOT and join the group.

262. CLOSE SHOT   CAIN THE SIXTH

CAIN THE SIXTH:
> Dere's de fool an' his monument, jes' like I said!

The crowd laughs again.

263.   CLOSE SHOT   ZEBA AND FLATFOOT
Zeba starts as she sees Cain the Sixth. Flatfoot is terrified.

264.   MED. CLOSE SHOT   GROUP AROUND ZEBA

CAIN THE SIXTH (to Zeba):
    Hello, honey.

ZEBA (frightened but smiling):
    Hello, sugah.

CAIN THE SIXTH (pleasantly):
    Ain' dat my ol' frien' Flatfoot wid you?

265.   CLOSE SHOT   ZEBA

ZEBA (smiling):
    Why, so 'tis! (To the others.) He's got a gun!

266.   MED. SHOT   CROWD
scattering.

CAIN THE SIXTH (with injured innocence, holding his
hands in the air):
    No, I ain't.

Zeba goes up to Cain the Sixth, whose hands are still in
the air. She lightly touches his side pockets, the front of
his coat, and the small of his back. Now she believes him.

ZEBA (relieved):
    I guess he ain't.

The crowd relaxes. Cain the Sixth drops his arms. He and
Flatfoot advance toward each other. Cain the Sixth ex-
tends his right hand.

CAIN THE SIXTH:
    Dey's no gun fo' my ol' frien' Flatfoot.

FLATFOOT (shaking Cain's hand):
>Hi, Cain. How de boy?

Cain the Sixth quickly pulls Flatfoot toward him, his left arm swings up to the center of Flatfoot's back.

CAIN THE SIXTH:
>I got a little knife fo' him.

267.   (ALTERNATE SHOTS)
CLOSE-UP   CAIN THE SIXTH'S HEAD AND BACK
in front of Flatfoot, who is facing the CAMERA. Here no detail of the stabbing is shown. We see the reaction on Flatfoot's face.

268.   CLOSE-UP   ZEBA
She is horrified.

269.   MED. SHOT   GROUP
Flatfoot has fallen to the ground, dead. Cain the Sixth looks at Zeba. He tosses the knife to the ground and holds out his hands to her. He is smiling. Zeba reconciles herself to the situation and meekly goes to him. She puts an arm around his neck.

ZEBA:
>You sho' take keer of me, honey.

CAIN THE SIXTH:
>Dat's caize I think yo' wo'th it. (He looks about.) It's all right, folks. I jes' had to do a little cleanin' up.

270.   CLOSE SHOT   NOAH
looking down at them.

NOAH:
>You bettah pray, you po' chillun.

271.   CLOSE SHOT   ZEBA

ZEBA:
   You mean you bettah pray. You bettah pray fo' rain.

272.   CLOSE SHOT   NOAH

NOAH:
   Dat's jes' what I ain't doin', sinners.

He looks down at his sleeve. We see a drop or two of water fall on it.

NOAH:
   Listen! (There is a distant roll of thunder.) Shem! Japheth!

273.   FULL SHOT   CROWD AROUND ARK
It is growing a little darker and the thunder is increasing. The people are looking up at the sky.

274.   MED. CLOSE SHOT   AROUND CAIN THE SIXTH AND ZEBA

CAIN THE SIXTH:
   Doggone, I believe it *is* gonter shower a little.

FIRST GAMBLER (holding out his hand):
   It do looks like rain.

WOMAN:
   I think I'll git on home. I got a new dress on.

The widow has raised her umbrella.

ZEBA:
   Me, too. I wants to keep lookin' nice fo' my sweet papa. (She pats Cain the Sixth's cheek.)

275.   MED. SHOT   NOAH ON THE DECK
He is looking down the gangplank. Increasing thunder comes over the scene. He lifts his arm and calls out:

NOAH:
Ham! Ham! Is you ready wid de animals?

HAM'S VOICE (in the distance):
Yassuh, Daddy. Dey all heah.

NOAH:
Tell 'em to line up!

There is a crash of thunder. Noah glances up.

NOAH:
God's give us his sign.

276.   CLOSER SHOT   NOAH
as he looks at the bottom of the paper and reads:

NOAH:
"Yellow jacks, yellow birds, and zebrays."

There is a flash of lightning over the SHOT and the off-scene choir begins singing "De Ol' Ark's A-Moverin'," continuing the song until the FADE OUT.

277.   FULL SHOT   CROWD
There is a flash of lightning and again a crash of thunder over the dispersing crowd.[32]

278.   CLOSE SHOT   GANGPLANK
Up the gangplank come two asses hauling a wagon in which are sectioned cages containing: two alligators, two alley cats, and two aardvarks. Each of the sections is plainly visible, as are the signs hanging outside denoting the contents. On the side of the ass nearer the CAMERA hangs a sign:

2 Asses

Tied to the wagon come two apes. If possible, the two small boxes should be attached to their paws. Next come two bullocks pulling a cage or wagon. In the wagon are: two badgers, two bullfrogs, and two buzzards. Following this are two bears. Behind them are two billy goats, with

little boxes hanging around their necks. Each of these animals is identified by a sign. As the billy goats pass the
CAMERA, we go to

279.   CLOSE SHOT OF BILLY GOAT NEARER CAMERA
       INSERT   CLOSE-UP BOX
       It is lettered:

                    2 Bull Weevils

       Behind the billy goats are two cows, followed by two
       camels, pulling another wagon in which are: two chip-
       munks, two coons, and two cranes.

280.   MED. SHOT   HAM ON HIS ZEBRA
       among the cows and the camels. He is cracking the whip
       and looking off scene. Behind him comes a section of the
       D's. We see two deer, two large dogs—St. Bernards—
       pulling a small wagon in which are some doves, and per-
       haps something else not visible.

       HAM:
           Everybody stay in line! Git back, you hogs! Git back
           amongst de *H*'s, behind de gee-raffes!

281.   CLOSE SHOT   HOGS
       scurrying past the two men gorillas that are drawing a
       big wagon. As the hogs enter, the gorillas stop and look
       around as a yell comes from off scene. Ham's attention is
       attracted by the sound.

       SHEM'S VOICE:
           Help me out yere!

282.   MED. SHOT   MELEE FROM ABOVE
       The rain continues over the SHOT. Ducks, sheep and lambs,
       chickens, a llama, two little ponies, two calves, spotted
       deer, seals, turkeys, mules, two pigs are all mixed up. In
       the middle stands Shem (and Japheth, if necessary). Ham
       arrives on the zebra.

SHEM (to Ham):
> Dey's a couple of weasels got loose!

283. MED. CLOSE SHOT   NOAH
Behind him on the deck, two oxen and two ostriches are
walking past.

NOAH (cupping his hands):
> Send 'em up any which-a-way!

284. JACKMAN SHOT OF THE LONG PARADE
The singing becomes louder. The rain is falling harder.
The ark is indistinctly seen in the rain, with the long line
of animals going up the gangplank. In the foreground lies
Flatfoot's body. Beside him is a shock of corn, which dis-
integrates under the impact of the rain. Flashes of lightning light the parade.

285. CLOSE SHOT   HAM, NOAH, SHEM, AND JAPHETH
standing on the deck, seen from below. The two zebras
are near. The men are hauling up the gangplank. The deluge has become so thick that they are hardly visible.

286–89. LONG SHOT   THE ARK   (MINIATURE)
It is in the distance, in the storm.

290. LONG SHOT   DISPERSING CLOUDS   (MINIATURE)
in front of the ark. The clouds go out, leaving a rainbow.
The rainbow FADES OUT, leaving the ark on a calm sea. A
dove flies from behind CAMERA toward ark.

291. CLOSE SHOT   AT RAIL OF ARK
Noah is standing behind rail watching the rain. The dove
flies into scene. Noah reaches out for dove and holds it
in his hand. The dove has an olive branch in its beak.

NOAH:
> Here's de li'l dove back wid greenery in his mouf'.

He looks over the rail at the countryside below.

292.　CLOSE SHOT　NOAH

NOAH:
　　Thank you, Lawd. Thank you very kindly. Amen.

The choir stops.

GOD'S VOICE:
　　Yo' welcome, Noah.

293.　MED. SHOT　GOD AND NOAH
God is now standing beside Noah.

NOAH:
　　O, Lawd, it's wonderful.

GOD (looking about):
　　I sort of like it. (He half glances at Noah.) I like de way you handled de ship, too.

NOAH:
　　Was you watchin', Lawd?

GOD:
　　Every minute.

NOAH (smiling, relieved):
　　What's de orders now?

GOD:
　　All de animals safe?

NOAH:
　　Dey fin'n' dandy, Lawd.

GOD:
　　Den open de starboard door an' leave 'em all out. You an' de fam'ly take all de seeds an' de sprouts an' begin plantin'. I'm startin' all over, Noah.

NOAH:
　　Yessuh, Lawd.

He disappears through the door.

294.　CLOSE-UP　GOD

GOD:
　　Gabriel, kin you spare a minute?

GABRIEL'S VOICE:
　　Yes, Lawd?

295.　MED. SHOT　FROM BELOW　LOOKING UP AT GOD AND
GABRIEL
who are leaning over the ark's rail.

GOD:
　　Well, it's did.

296.　LONG SHOT　STOCK　A LUSH COUNTRYSIDE
On it there are little lakes and ponds that will give the
suggestion of the vanishing flood.

297.　CLOSE SHOT　GOD AND GABRIEL

GABRIEL (casually):
　　So I take notice.

GOD:
　　Don' seem to set you up much.

GABRIEL:
　　Well, Lawd—'tain't none of my business.

GOD:
　　Co'se it ain't. It's my business. 'Twas my idea. An'
　　every bit is my business 'n' nobody else's. You know
　　dis thing's turned into quite a proposition. (A bird
　　lights on God's shoulder.) I only hope it's goin' to
　　wukk out all right.

　　　　　　　　　　　　　　　　　　　　　FADE OUT

THIS SCENE TO BE CUT IN AFTER ARK SEQUENCE   SCHOOLROOM

MYRTLE:
> An' did it work out?

DESHEE:
> No it didn't. De minute de Lawd turned his back, dere dey was, bad as ever.

CARLISLE:
> What did de poor Lawd do den?

DESHEE:
> Oh, he let 'em go 'long fo' a spell. Den one day he looked down from heaven, an' he don't like what he see a-tall.

FADE IN

298.   INT. GOD'S OFFICE   MED. CLOSE SHOT   DAY
TWO WOMEN CLEANERS

A whistle something like that of a skyrocket causes the cleaners to look up. They listen. The whistle dies away and there is a distant boom.

FIRST CLEANER:
> Dat's de fo'ty-six' thunde'bolt since breakfast. De Lawd mus' be mad fo' sho' dis mo'nin'.

SECOND CLEANER:
> Whereat's he pitchin' 'em?

FIRST CLEANER:
> Dey boun' fo' de earth.

SECOND CLEANER:
> You mean dat little ol' dreenin' place?

FIRST CLEANER:
> Carrie, don't you know de earth is de new scandal? Everybody's talkin' 'bout it. De Lawd is riled as kin be at dat measly little planet. Or I should say de scum dat's on it.

SECOND CLEANER (as if the first cleaner had been blasphemous):

> Dat's mankind down dere.

FIRST CLEANER:

> Dey mus' be scum too, to git de Lawd so wukked up.

There is another whistle and a distant boom.

SECOND CLEANER:

> He's lettin' 'em feel de wrath. Ain't dat a shame to plague de Lawd dat way?

FIRST CLEANER:

> Dey been beggin' fo' what dey're gittin'. My brother flew down to bring up a saint de other day an' he say from what he see mos' of de population down dere has made de debbil king an' dey wukkin' in three shifts fo' him. Dem human bein's 'd make anybody bile ovah.

299.   CLOSE SHOT   SECOND CLEANER

wiping the edge of the desk, which is chipped a little.

SECOND CLEANER:

> Why won't de Lawd let us ladies fix up his office nice? Wouldn't take a minute to make dis desk gold plated.

300.   MED. SHOT   THE TWO CLEANERS

FIRST CLEANER:

> I guess he keeps de private office plain an' simple on purpose.

301.   CLOSE-UP   FIRST CLEANER

as she continues:

FIRST CLEANER:

> Everythin' else in heaven's so fine an' gran', maybe

every now an' den he jes' gits sick an' tired of de glory.

GOD'S VOICE:
Good mo'nin', daughters.

The first cleaner looks off scene quickly.

302.   MED. SHOT   OFFICE
God is standing in the doorway. Gabriel, carrying a ledger under his arm, is behind him.

SECOND CLEANER:
Good mo'nin', Lawd. We all finished.

God walks into the room as the cleaners pick up their utensils and pass Gabriel, who is entering.

CLEANERS (together):
Good mo'nin', Gabriel.

GABRIEL (absently, watching God):
Good mo'nin', sisters.

God goes to the window. The cleaners exit.

303.   CLOSE-UP   GOD
looking down from the window.

GOD:
What's de total?

304.   MED. CLOSE SHOT   GOD AND GABRIEL

GABRIEL (consulting his book):
Eighteen thousand nine hund'ed an' sixty fo' de mo'nin'. Dat's including de village wid de fo'tune tellers. Dey certainly kin breed fas'.

GOD:
Dey displeases me. Dey displeases me greatly. Look at dem dere. Squirmin' an' fightin' an' bearin' false witness. Why did I ever make 'em?

GABRIEL:
> Should I git mo' thunde'bolts?

GOD (looking down):
> No. Dey don' do de trick.

305. MED. SHOT OFFICE
God walks away from the window and sits down in his swivel chair.

GOD:
> It's gotta be somethin' else.

306. CLOSE SHOT GABRIEL

GABRIEL:
> How would it be if you was to doom 'em all ag'in, like dat time you sent down de flood? I bet dat'd make 'em min'.

307. MED. SHOT THE TWO

GOD:
> You see how much good de flood did.

GABRIEL:
> Well, how 'bout cleanin' up de whole mess of 'em an sta'tin' all ovah ag'in wid some new kin' of animal?

GOD:
> An' admit I'm licked?

GABRIEL:
> No, of co'se not, Lawd.

GOD:
> It ain' right fo' me to give up tryin' to do somethin' wid 'im. Doggone, mankin' *mus'* be all right at de core or else why did I ever bother wid 'im in de fust place?

GABRIEL:
> I jes hate to see you worryin' 'bout it, Lawd.

308.   CLOSE SHOT   GOD

GOD:

Gabe, dey ain't nothin' wo'th while anywhere dat
don't cause somebody some worryin'. I ain't never
tol' you de trouble I had gittin' things sta'ted up
yere. Dat's a story in itself.

309.   CLOSE-UP   GABRIEL

He looks almost frightened by the idea.

                                          CUT BACK TO:

310.   CLOSE SHOT   GOD

GOD:

No, suh, de more I keep on bein' de Lawd de more
I know I got to keep improvin' things. De main
trouble is mankin' takes up so much of my time. He
ought to be able to help hisself a little. (An idea
strikes him.) Hey, dere! I think I got it!

311.   MED. CLOSE SHOT   THE TWO

Gabriel is now standing a little closer to God.

GABRIEL:

What's de news?

GOD:

Gabriel, have you noticed dat every now an' den
mankin' turns out some pretty good specimens?

GABRIEL:

Dey wouldn't come flying up yere if dey hadn't been.

GOD:

Yes, suh, doggone it, de good man is de man dat
keeps busy. I really put de fust one down dere to take
keer o' dat garden an' den I let him go ahead an' do
nothin' but git into mischief. (He rises.) Dat's it! He
ain't *built* jes' to fool aroun' an' not do nothin'.
Gabe, I'm gonter try a new scheme. (Softly, not looking at Gabriel.) Round up Abraham, Isaac, an' Jacob.

VOICE:
> We'll git 'em, Lawd.

GABRIEL (eagerly):
> What's de scheme, Lawd?

GOD:
> I'll tell you later. (Crossing toward the window.) You go tell dem to put dem bolts back in de boxes. I ain't gonter use dem ag'in fo' a while.

GABRIEL:
> Okay, Lawd. (He starts for the door.)

GOD:
> Was you goin' anywhere near de big pit?

GABRIEL:
> I could go.

GOD:
> Lean ovah de brink an' tell ol' Satan he's jes' a plain fool if he thinks he kin beat anybody as big as me.

GABRIEL (smiling):
> Yessuh, Lawd. Den I'll spit right in his eye.

He exits.

312.   CLOSE SHOT   GOD   SHOOTING THROUGH WINDOW

GOD:
> Dat new polish on de sun makes it powerful hot. (Softly.) Let it be jes' a little bit cooler. (He feels the air.) Dat's nice.

A knock comes over the SHOT.

GOD (turning):
> Come in.

313.   MED. SHOT   ABRAHAM, ISAAC, AND JACOB   ANGLE INCLUDING GOD

They are very old men, and they suggest their three generations, the beard of Abraham being the longest and whitest. They have wings that are not quite so big as those of the native angels.

ISAAC:

> Sorry we so long comin', Lawd. But Pappy an' me had to take de boy—(he indicates Jacob) ovah to git him a can of wing ointment.

GOD:

> What was de matter, son?

JACOB (shrugging his shoulders):

> Dey was chafin' me a little. Dey fine now, thank you, Lawd.

GOD:

> Dat's good. Sit down an' make yo'selves comf'table.

The three murmur "Thank you, Lawd" as they seat themselves.

GOD:

> You is about de three best boys of one fam'ly dat's come up yeah since I made little apples. An' I've decided to turn ovah to yo' descendants de biggest an' best piece of property in de whole world. Now you boys know what's down dere. Where do you think it's at?

The three heads go together in conference.

ABRAHAM:

> If you ask us, Lawd, we don't think dey come any better dan de land of Canaan.

GOD:

> Yes, dat's a likely neighborhood. (Musingly.) Dey's Philistines dere now; we'll clean dem up.

314.   CLOSE SHOT   THE THREE OLD MEN   SMILING AT EACH OTHER.[33]

315.   CLOSE-UP   GOD

GOD:
   Now who do you think is de bes' one of yo' people
   to put in charge down dere?

316.   CLOSE SHOT   THE THREE OLD MEN

ISAAC:
   Does you want de brainiest or de holiest, Lawd?

GOD'S VOICE:
   I want de holiest. I'll make him brainy.

The men appreciate the miracle.

ISAAC:
   Well, if you want A-number-one goodness, Lawd, I
   don't know where you'll git more satisfaction dan in
   a great-great-great-great-grandson of mine.

316A.   CLOSE-UP   GOD

GOD (smiling unnoticed by them):
   Where's he at?

316B.   CLOSE-UP   ISAAC

ISAAC:
   I b'lieve he's in de sheep business ovah in Midian
   Parish. Ovah in Egypt, he—he killed a man dat was
   abusin' our people in de brick wukks. You know ol'
   King Pharaoh's got all our people in bondage.

317.   CLOSE-UP   GOD

GOD:
   I heerd of it. (Sharply.) Who did you think put dem
   dere?

318.   CLOSE SHOT   ABRAHAM, ISAAC, AND JACOB
They lower their heads in submission.

GOD'S VOICE (over SHOT):
> Dat's all right. I'm gonter take dem out of it.

They look up, relieved. The choir begins softly to sing "My Lord's A-Writin' All de Time."

319.   MED. SHOT   GOD AND THE THREE OLD MEN
God rises. So do the others.

GOD:
> I'm gonter turn ovah de whole land of Canaan to you. You know who's gonter lead dem dere? Yo' great-great-great-great-grandson. (Slyly.) His name is Moses, ain't it?

ISAAC (astounded):
> Yes, Lawd.

GOD (confidentially):
> I been noticin' him. An' I know he ain't a bad boy.

ABRAHAM:
> It's quite a favor fo' de fam'ly, Lawd.

GOD (crosses to the window):
> Dat's why I tol' you. You see, it so happens I love yo' fam'ly, an' I delights to honor it.

The three men, delighted, smile at each other.

320.   CLOSE SHOT   GOD
looking down through the window.

GOD:
> I'm comin' down to see you, Moses, an' dis time my scheme's *got* to wukk.

The choir continues, covering the DISSOLVE.

> DISSOLVE TO:

321.   MED. SHOT   ELEVATED SPACE BEFORE THE OPENING OF A CAVE
There is a sharp decline away from this space, and below,

perhaps ten or twelve feet, we see sheep grazing. The choir continues. Moses is seated, eating some lunch from a basket in his lap. Zipporah, his wife, stands beside him. He is about forty, Zipporah somewhat younger. They are dressed inconspicuously. Moses stutters slightly when he speaks. It is darker in the immediate neighborhood of Moses. The choir stops. Moses looks up to see Zipporah smiling at him.

MOSES:
> You is a funny wife, Zipporah. What you smilin' at?

ZIPPORAH:
> Caize you enjoyin' yo'self, Moses.

322.   CLOSE SHOT   MOSES AND ZIPPORAH
Moses is finishing his meal.

ZIPPORAH (looking about her):
> Why you suppose it's so dark yere today? Dey's no rain in de air.

MOSES:
> Seems like it's jes' around dis cave.

ZIPPORAH:
> Look, de sun's on yo' brother Aaron an' de sheep.

Moses waves his hand to his brother Aaron off scene.

323.   LONG SHOT   AARON AND THE SHEEP   FROM MOSES'S ANGLE
showing them in a sunlit field.

324.   MED. SHOT   MOSES AND ZIPPORAH

ZIPPORAH:
> Looks like good weather over toward Egypt. Do you s'pose it could be de Lawd warnin' you dat dey's 'Gyptians hangin' 'roun'?

MOSES:
>Dey may have fo'gotten all about dat killin' by now.
>Dey got a new pharaoh down dere.

ZIPPORAH:
>An' I hear he's jes' as mean to yo' people as his pappy
>was. I wouldn't put it pas' him to send soljahs all de
>way up yere fo' you.

MOSES:
>Well, de Lawd's looked after me so far, I don't 'spect
>him to fall down on me now. You better be gittin'
>home.

ZIPPORAH (picking up the basket):
>I'll be worryin' 'bout you.

MOSES (kissing her):
>Well, 'parently de Lawd ain't. (She starts away.) He
>knows I'm safe as kin be.

Zipporah leaves the scene.[34]

325.　CLOSE-UP　MOSES

MOSES (looking up at the sky):
>Dat's funny. De sun seems to be shinin' everyplace
>but right yere. Why ain't dey no cloud dere?

GOD'S VOICE:
>Caize I want it to be like dat, Moses.

MOSES:
>Who's dat?

GOD'S VOICE:
>I'm de Lawd, Moses.

MOSES (laughing):
>Dat's what you say. Dis yere shadow may be de
>Lawd's wukk—(looking about) but dat voice soun'
>pretty much to me like a little echo, or somethin'.

GOD'S VOICE:
Den keep yo' eyes open, son.

Moses turns around, and beside him a large turkeyberry bush in the foreground turns into flame.

326. CLOSE SHOT   TURKEYBERRY BUSH
glowing. The flames subside, and the bush is intact.

GOD'S VOICE:
Maybe you notice de bush ain't burned up?

327. CLOSE SHOT   MOSES
looking at the bush. He touches the fresh green leaves.

MOSES (softly):
Dat's de truth.

He is awed but not frightened.

GOD'S VOICE:
Now you believe me?

MOSES:
Yessuh, Lawd. It's wonderful.

GOD'S VOICE (a little more loudly):
No, it ain't, Moses. It's jes' a trick.

Moses turns about sharply, recognizing the direction of the voice.

328. MED. CLOSE SHOT   GOD AND MOSES

MOSES:
'Scuse me doubtin' you, Lawd. I always had de feelin' you wuz takin' keer of me, but I never 'spected you'd fin' time to talk wid me pussunly. (He looks back at the bush.) Dat was a good trick, Lawd. I seen some good ones, but dat was de beatenest.

GOD:

You gonter see lots bigger tricks dan dat, Moses. In fac', yo' gonter perfo'm dem.

MOSES:

Me? I'm gonter be a tricker?

GOD:

Yes.

MOSES:

An' do magic? Lawd, my mouf ain't got de quick talk to go wid it.

GOD:

It'll come to you now.

Moses touches his mouth, feeling a change in its formation. From now on Moses speaks with easy fluency.

MOSES:

Is I goin' wid a circus?

GOD:

Yo' is goin' down to Egypt, Moses, an' lead my people out of bondage. To do dat I'm gonter make you de bes' tricker in de worl'.

MOSES:

Egypt! You know I killed a man dere, Lawd. Won't dey kill me?

GOD:

Not when dey see yo' tricks. You ain't skeered, is you?

MOSES (simply and bravely):

No, suh, Lawd.

GOD:

Den yere's what I'm gonter do. I'm sick an' tired o' de way ol' King Pharaoh's treatin' my chillun, Moses, an' you're goin' to lead dem away. Yo' gonter lead

dem out of Egypt an' across de river Jordan. It's gonter take a long time, an' it ain't gonter be no excur-
sion trip. Yo' gonter wukk awful hard fo' somethin'
yo' gonter fin' when de trip's over.

MOSES:

What's dat, Lawd?

GOD:

De land of Canaan.

MOSES:

Co'se ol' King Pharaoh he'll say no.

GOD:

Dat's where de tricks come in. Dey tell me he's awful
fond of tricks.

MOSES:

I hear dat's *all* he's fond of. Dey say if you cain't take
a rabbit out of a hat you cain't even git in to see him.

GOD:

Wait'll you see de tricks you an' me's gonter show
him.

MOSES:

Doggone! Huh, Lawd?

GOD:

Yes, suh. Now de fust trick—

MOSES:

Jes' a minute, Lawd. I wanter do jes' like you tell me
to. But I know it's gonter take a little time to learn all
dat quick talkin'. Cain't my brother Aaron go wid
me? He's a good man.

GOD:

I was gonter have him help you wid de Exodus. I
guess he can watch, too.

The choir softly begins singing "Go Down, Moses."

MOSES:
> I'll call 'im.

He turns as if to shout.

GOD:
> Wait. I'll *bring* 'im. (Softly.) Aaron!

329. MED. SHOT   NEAR CAVE
Aaron is standing beside Moses, who looks at him in sur-
prise. Aaron is a little taller than Moses and slightly older.
He, too, is dressed like a field hand.

AARON (not knowing what has happened to him):
> Hey!

MOSES (softly patting Aaron's shoulder):
> It's all right.

GOD:
> Don't worry, son. (Aaron sees God.) I'm jes' showin'
> some tricks. Bringin' you yere was one of dem. Now
> den, see dis yere rod? Looks like a ordinary walking
> stick, don't it?

MOSES:
> Yes, Lawd.

330. CLOSE SHOT   GOD

GOD:
> Well, it ain't no ordinary walking stick, caize look.
> (CAMERA STARTS TO PAN DOWN SLOWLY during the
> following speech.) When I lays it down on de
> ground—

God's arm is withdrawn from the SHOT. The stick slowly
turns into a snake. Over the SHOT the singing reaches fortissimo and then stops, as the CAMERA PULLS AWAY TO A

[331–34.] MED. SHOT   THRONE ROOM OF OL' KING PHARAOH
The throne room suggests a Negro lodge room. King

Pharaoh enters. The crowd bows as he makes his way to
the throne.

PHARAOH:

> We open de meetin' wid de repo't of my confidential
> magician.

The confidential magician steps forward.

PHARAOH:

> Mo'nin', professor. What's de news? How's de killin'
> of de babies 'mongst de Hebrews comin' along?

MAGICIAN (smiling):

> Jes' like you ordered. We killed about a thousand las'
> night. Dat's pretty good.

PHARAOH:

> Dat's fair. But I fin' I ain't satisfied, though.

MAGICIAN:

> But dey ain't nothin' meaner dan killin' de babies,
> king.

PHARAOH:

> Oh, dey *mus'* be sump'n. Put yo' brains on it.

MAGICIAN:

> Tell you what I kin do. All de Hebrews dat ain't in
> the buryin' grounds is laborin' in de brick wukks.

PHARAOH:

> Yeah?

MAGICIAN:

> How would it be to take de straw away from 'em an'
> tell 'em dey gotta turn out as many bricks as usual.
> Ain't dat nasty?

PHARAOH:

> Naw, but go try it fo' de time bein'. Wait a minute.
> If anyone say he cain't make bricks dat way, chop off
> his hands.

MAGICIAN:
Now we gittin' somewhere.

He leaves the scene.

PHARAOH:
Any newcomers today?

A MAN:
Jes' dese two yere.

Moses and Aaron step forth from the crowd. They are dressed in the simple Sunday clothes of field hands.

PHARAOH:
What you boys got to demonstrate?

MOSES:
We got a wonderful walkin' stick!

PHARAOH:
What's it do?

MOSES:
You kin see fo' yo'self.

He lays it on the step of the throne.

335.   CLOSE-UP   CONFEDERATE GENERAL
GENERAL:
It made de roun' trip!

336.   CLOSE SHOT   PHARAOH
with Moses and Aaron in the foreground. The murmur of the others continues over the SHOT.

PHARAOH:
You *is* good trickers! How come you ain't never showed up at de palace befo'?

MOSES:
We jes' come to town, ol' King Pharaoh.

Pharaoh looks at them a moment and smiles.

154

PHARAOH:
> What's yo' name?

MOSES:
> Mine's Moses. Dis is my brother Aaron.

PHARAOH (startled; angrily):
> Hebrews! (The word is echoed by the others.) Is you
> Hebrews?

MOSES:
> Yes, suh.

PHARAOH (angrily):
> Put 'em to de sword!

337. MED. SHOT THRONE ROOM
Aaron swings the rod in a circle above the heads of himself and Moses.

MOSES:
> Keep outside dat circle!

The soldiers, with old-fashioned sabers and swords, such
as are carried by officers of Negro lodges, rush to Moses
and Aaron as the others fall back.

338. CLOSE SHOT ONE SOLDIER
about to strike. The sword hits the edge of the imaginary
circle and stops. He looks at his raised hand to see what
has stopped it, his arm quivering.

339. MED. SHOT SIX SOLDIERS
all halted in the same way.

340. CLOSE SHOT PHARAOH

PHARAOH:
> What's de idea yere?

341.   CLOSE SHOT   MOSES

MOSES (smiling; calmly):
We is magicians, ol' King Pharaoh.

342.   CLOSE SHOT   PHARAOH

PHARAOH:
Well, we got some yere, too. Where is de head tricker of de land of Egypt?

343.   CLOSE SHOT   HEAD MAGICIAN
who is a villainous old man.

HEAD MAGICIAN:
I'se yere.

344.   MED. SHOT   GROUP AROUND MAGICIAN
at the left of the throne. The head magician walks slowly toward Moses and Aaron, through a path made by the separation of the crowd.

345.   CLOSE SHOT   MOSES AND AARON
as the head magician enters the SHOT.

PHARAOH:
Now we'll see who's got de bes' magic. Go ahead. Give dese boys gri-gri.

The head magician smiles and, with the thumb and third finger of each hand, pulls away from the center of a piece of string.

346.   CLOSE SHOT   MOSES
casually looking upward, while pointing a finger at the string in the magician's hand.

347.   CLOSE-UP   HEAD MAGICIAN
The string breaks. He drops the pieces and wiggles his fingers as if they were tingling. The laughter of Moses

and Aaron comes over the SHOT. The head magician is startled and terrified.

348.　MED. SHOT　MOSES, AARON, PHARAOH, AND MAGICIAN
and one or two others. Moses and Aaron are laughing heartily.

PHARAOH:
　　What's de matter? Dey laughin' at you!

HEAD MAGICIAN:
　　Somethin' got in de way of de spell.

PHARAOH:
　　You mean dey got even *you* whupped?

349.　CLOSE SHOT　FIRST WIZARD
leaning over Pharaoh's shoulder.

FIRST WIZARD (slowly, registering awe at the implication of the power of Moses and Aaron):
　　Dey got a new kind of magic.

350.　CLOSE SHOT　HEAD MAGICIAN

MAGICIAN:
　　It's got 'lectricity in it!

351.　MED. SHOT　GROUP AROUND PHARAOH

PHARAOH (gently):
　　Hm, dat may make it a little diff'rent. (To Moses.) You boys is okay. I s'pose you know I'm a fool fo' conjurin'. If a man kin show me some tricks I ain't seen, I goes out of my way to do him a favor.

MOSES:
　　Any favor?

PHARAOH (airily):
　　Name yo' fancy.

MOSES (softly):
Let de Hebrew chillun go!

There is an uproar.

AD LIB:
Listen to 'im! He's got nerve! I never in my life! My
goodness! He's gettin' sassy!

352.   CLOSE SHOT   PHARAOH

PHARAOH (rising):
What did you say?

353.   CLOSE SHOT   MOSES

MOSES:
Let de Hebrew chillun go!35

354.   MED. CLOSE SHOT   GROUP AROUND PHARAOH

PHARAOH:
Don' you know de Hebrews is my slaves? I hates
'em! All week we been killin' de babies. An' it ain't
five minutes since I give de orders to chop off dere
hands if dey cain't make bricks widout straw. (With
a sinister smile.) Let's see some mo' of yo' tricks.

355.   OMITTED

356.   MED. CLOSE SHOT   PHARAOH, MOSES, AND AARON

PHARAOH (with a sinister smile):
Let's see some mo' of yo' tricks.

357–60. OMITTED

361.   MED. SHOT   MOSES, AARON, PHARAOH, AND OTHERS IN
THE VICINITY

MOSES:
I got one mo' trick up my sleeve which I didn't aim

to wukk unless I had to. Caize when I does *dis* one,
I cain't undo it.

PHARAOH:

Wukk it an' I'll trick you right back. You one of de
bes' trickers I ever seen, Moses, but I kin outtrick
you any time of de day.

MOSES:

It ain't only me dat's goin' to wukk dis trick. It's me
an de Lawd.

PHARAOH:

WHO?

MOSES:

De Lawd God of Israel.

PHARAOH:

I kin outtrick you an' de Lawd too!

MOSES (angrily):

Now you done it, ol' King Pharaoh! You been mean
to de Lawd's people, an de Lawd's been easy on you
caize you didn' know no better. You been givin' me
a lot of say-so-and-no-do-so, an' I didn' min' dat.
But now you've got to braggin' dat you's better dan
de Lawd, an' dat's too many.

PHARAOH:

You talk like a preacher, an' I never did like preachers.

MOSES:

You ain't goin' to like it any better when I strikes
down de oldes' boy in every one of yo' people's
houses!

362.   LONGER SHOT   TAKING IN MORE PEOPLE
They are terrified by Moses's threat. Pharaoh rises from
his throne.

PHARAOH:

Listen, I'm Pharaoh!

363.　CLOSE SHOT　AT THRONE

The two wizards and a young attendant with a peacock fan look at Pharaoh in dumb anguish, as he speaks. The first wizard puts his arm around the boy attendant's shoulder.

PHARAOH:

I do de strikin' yere. I strikes down my enemies, an' dere's no one in all Egypt kin kill who he wants to, 'ceptin' me.

There is a murmur of protest.

FIRST WIZARD:

No, no! Let 'em go, Pharaoh!

Pharaoh turns angrily to the wizard.

PHARAOH:

You heard my word.

364.　MED. CLOSE SHOT　GROUP AROUND MOSES

Moses and Aaron are looking upward again.

PHARAOH:

Now, no mo' tricks or I'll—

MOSES:

Lawd, you'll have to do it, I guess. Aaron, lift de rod.

Aaron starts to lift the rod.[36]

365.　CLOSE-UP　PHARAOH'S FACE

His eyes follow the lifting of the rod. Over the SHOT comes a thunderclap and the terrific screaming of the assemblage. Pharaoh's jaw drops. He looks down toward his feet. The CAMERA TRUCKS BACK A LITTLE TO A

366.　CLOSE SHOT　PHARAOH

We see the body of the young fan-bearer lying at Pharaoh's feet. On his knees beside it is the wizard, looking up at Pharaoh piteously. Pharaoh turns to look at the rest of the room.

367. FULL SHOT THRONE ROOM FROM PHARAOH'S ANGLE
On the floor, with the huddled group of relatives about them, are five or six dead youths and children. Aaron is slowly lowering the rod.

368. CLOSE SHOT PHARAOH

PHARAOH:
What you done yere? Where's my boy?

369. MED. SHOT AT DOOR
Some soldiers are opening the door to the throne room. Four soldiers enter, carrying a litter on which is the body of a boy of twelve. The CAMERA TRUCKS BEFORE THEM as the crowd makes way for their passage toward the throne. They stop at the throne, and the young soldier at the foot of the litter looks up.

370. CLOSE SHOT AT LITTER

SOLDIER:
King Pharaoh. Yere is yo' boy.

371. CLOSE SHOT PHARAOH
He drops his scepter and staggers down the steps of the throne to the litter, which is at the foot of the dais. Pharaoh kneels beside the dead boy.

PHARAOH:
Oh, my son! My fine son!

372. CLOSE SHOT MOSES

MOSES (gently):
I'm sorry, Pharaoh, but you cain't fight de Lawd. Will you let his people go?

PHARAOH:
Let dem go.

A deep baritone voice comes over the SHOT singing "Go Down, Moses." The CAMERA STAYS on Pharaoh for the first two lines, to the end of " 'way down in Egypt land."

373. WIDER ANGLE
Moses and Aaron slowly turn and start toward the door. The crowd makes way for them. The singer's voice continues over the SHOT.

374. CLOSE TRUCK SHOT   MOSES'S AND AARON'S LEGS
as they pass two or three of the dead first-born on the floor. Crouching beside the corpses are the figures of the sorrowing men and women.[37] As the voices reach the end of "let my people go! ",

DISSOLVE TO:

375. CLOSE SHOT   MANY LEGS
marching on a dusty road. CAMERA TRUCKING BEFORE THEM. Over the SHOT comes the sound of the full choir singing "I'm No Ways Weary." CAMERA RISES IN AN ELEVATED SHOT TO A POSITION TWO OR THREE FEET ABOVE THE HEADS OF THE NEAREST MARCHERS,[38] disclosing:

376. FULL SHOT   MARCHERS
The screen is completely filled with the marchers advancing on a treadmill toward the CAMERA—men, women, and children, dressed in burlap robes, many of them carrying bundles. Smaller children are on the shoulders of the adults. Their faces are turned slightly upward. All are singing. The song reaches fortissimo.

377. FULL SHOT   MARCHERS   FROM A SIDE VIEW
The marchers go past the CAMERA. The song continues. Three sharp bugle notes come over the SHOT. The marchers stop. There are ad lib cries of:

AD LIB:

> What's de matter? Why do we stop? 'Tain't sundown yet! What dey blowin' fo'?

Over the SHOT we hear from a distance the cry "Moses! Somethin's happened to Moses!" a young man in the foreground turns to those near him.

YOUNG MAN:

> It's Moses! Somethin's happened to Moses!

The sounds continue to the left of the scene, with repetitions of "Moses! Somethin's happened to Moses!"

378. MED. FULL SHOT HEAD OF THE PROCESSION MOSES AND AARON

The marchers have all halted. Moses and Aaron are now old men with long flowing beards. Terror is on the faces of those around him as Moses feebly sits down on a stone by the roadside.

379. CLOSE SHOT MOSES AND AARON

AARON:

> What's de matter, Moses?

MOSES:

> I is so weary all at onct, Aaron.

380–81. OMITTED

382. MED. CLOSE SHOT MOSES AND THOSE NEARBY

MOSES:

> De Lawd said I'd do it. He said I was to show you de Promised Land. Fo' fo'ty years I been leadin' you— out o' Egypt, past Sinai, an' through de wilderness. I cain't fall down on you now!

AARON:

> It's been a hard day.

MOSES:
>De sun's gone down, ain't it?

383.   MED. SHOT   AARON AND THOSE NEAR HIM
looking at the sunset.

AARON:
>De sun ain't gone down, brother.

384.   CLOSE SHOT   MOSES AND AARON AND THOSE NEARBY

MOSES:
>No, it's my eyes.

There is a murmuring groan from the marchers.

MOSES:
>Oh, Lawd, dey cain't have a blind man leadin' 'em!
>Aaron, does you think it's de time he said?

AARON (putting his arm around Moses):
>How you mean?

MOSES:
>He said I could lead 'em to de Jordan; dat I'd *see* de
>Promised Land, an' dat's all de furder I could go, on
>'count I broke de laws. Little while back I thought I
>*did* see a river ahead, an' a pretty land on de odder
>side.

There are shouts of:

AD LIB:
>Here dey are! Here come de scouts!, etc.

Aaron and the others look off scene.[39]

385–87.   OMITTED

388.   MED. CLOSE SHOT   MOSES, AARON, AND OTHERS

MOSES:
>Where's de young leader of de troops? Where's
>Joshua?

AARON:

> Yeah he come.

Joshua enters the SHOT running.

MOSES:

> What's all de shoutin' 'bout, Joshua?

JOSHUA (excitedly):

> De scouts is back wid de news. De River Jordan is right ahead of us, an' Jericho is jes' on de other side. Moses, we'se dere!

A great shout goes up from all the listeners except Moses and Aaron.

389.   FULL SHOT   CROWD
coming closer to Moses.

AD LIB:

> Hoo-ray! De kingdom's comin'! De Lawd be praised!

Against the skyline we see their hands go up in the air, and the torn banners of burlap waving over the heads of the jubilant throng.

390.   CLOSE SHOT   MOSES AND GROUP

MOSES:

> Joshua, you gotta take de city of Jericho befo' sundown.

JOSHUA:

> But it's a big city, Father Moses, wid walls all 'round it. We ain't got enough men.

MOSES:

> Move up to de walls wid our people. Tell de priests to go wid you wid de rams' horns. You start marchin' 'round dem walls, an' den—

Moses is staring straight ahead of himself, as though clairvoyant. Then his eyes drop; his miraculous vision has faded.

JOSHUA:

Yes, suh.

MOSES (now the simple old man again):

De Lawd'll take charge of you, jes' as he's took charge ev'y time I've led you against a city. He ain't never failed, has he? (He looks around.)

391.   MED. SHOT   INCLUDING THOSE NEARBY

Their eyes are lifted to heaven.

SEVERAL:

No, Father Moses.

MOSES:

An' he ain't gonter fail us now.

He makes an effort to rise, and is assisted by Joshua and Aaron, each holding one of his arms in the air. The others kneel. The three standing figures are half-silhouetted against the northern skyline.

MOSES:

Oh, Lawd, I'm turnin' over our brave young men to you, caize I know you don't want me to lead 'em any furder.

392.   CLOSE-UP   MOSES

MOSES:

Jes' like you said, I've got to de Jordan but I cain't git over it. An' yere dey goin' now to take de city of Jericho. In a little while dey'll be marchin' roun' it. Would you please be so good as to tell 'em what to do? Amen.

393. FULL SHOT   CROWD

rising. Moses sinks feebly. Joshua and Aaron assist him to his seat on the stone.

MOSES:

Go ahead. Give de signal. You's gonter move on wid e'vythin'.

Joshua raises his sword, which flashes in the sun, and instantly a trumpet is heard. There is a general movement—picking up of bundles, shouldering of children, etc., for the resumption of the march.

394. MED. CLOSE SHOT   MOSES AND GROUP

MOSES:

You camp fo' de night in de city of Jericho.

JOSHUA:

What about you, Father Moses?

MOSES:

I'm stayin' behind. De Lawd's got his plans fo' me. Soun' de signal to march!

Joshua's sword flashes in the sun again. Another trumpet call is heard. The voices of the singers resume "I'm No Ways Weary," as Joshua dashes off, singing.

MOSES (to Aaron):

Take care of de ark of de covenant, Aaron.

AARON:

I will, Good-by.

MOSES:

Good-by.

395. CLOSE-UP   MOSES

The song comes over the SHOT. Moses sits staring in front of him as young hands and old hands pat his shoulder as the company passes him.

MOSES (murmuring):
> Good-by, my chillun.

The last of the marchers move out of the SHOT. Moses looks up after them.

396-97. LONG SHOT THE MARCHERS
as they recede. Nearest the CAMERA are the laggards: a small child in a wheelbarrow and a tiny rear guard of soldiers. The line stretches over a winding country toward a sinking sun. The singing grows softer.

398. CLOSE-UP MOSES
The singing comes softly OVER the SHOT.

MOSES:
> Yere I is, Lawd. De chillun is goin' into de Promised Land. You's with me, ain't you Lawd?

GOD'S VOICE:
> Co'se I is.

Moses looks up. (The singing stops.)

MOSES:
> I guess I'm through, Lawd. Jes' like you said I'd be when I broke de tablets of de law.

399. CLOSE SHOT GOD AND MOSES

GOD:
> Jes' what was it I said to you, Moses? Do you remember?

MOSES:
> I couldn't go into de Promised Land.

GOD:
> Moses, you angered me once, dat's true. But you been a good man. Now you gonter have your *own* Promised Land. I been gittin' it ready fo' you, fo' a long time. Kin you stan' up?[40]

MOSES (rising):
> Yessuh, Lawd.

GOD:

> Come on, I'll show it to you. We goin' up dis hill to
> git to it. It's a million times nicer dan de land of
> Canaan.

400.   MED. SHOT   GOD AND MOSES

They start climbing a hill. God's arm is around Moses's
shoulder. Moses leans a little heavily on his staff. The distant song has now stopped.

MOSES:
> I cain't hardly see.

GOD (lightly):
> Don't worry. Dat's jes' caize you so old.

They plod upward a few more steps. Moses stops
suddenly.

MOSES:
> Oh!

401.   CLOSE SHOT   GOD AND MOSES

GOD:
> What's de matter?

MOSES:

> We cain't be doin' dis! I fo'got all about Joshua an'
> de fightin' men!

GOD:
> What about 'em?

MOSES:

> Dey's marchin' on Jericho. I tol' 'em to march aroun'
> de walls an' den de Lawd would be dere to tell 'em
> what to do.

GOD:
> Dat's all right. I'se dere.

402.   CLOSE-UP   MOSES

MOSES:
> Den who's dis helpin' me up de hill?

GOD'S VOICE:
> Yo' faith, yo' God.

MOSES:
> An' is you over dere helpin' dem, too, Lawd? Is you gonter tell dem poor chillun what to do?

403.   CLOSE SHOT   GOD AND MOSES

GOD:
> Co'se I is. Listen, Moses, I'll show you how I'm helpin' dem.

God lifts his right arm to the level of his shoulder, palm downward, and looks off scene.

404.   LONG SHOT   THE CITY OF JERICHO, WITH THE RIVER JORDAN IN THE MIDDLE DISTANCE   (MINIATURE)
seen from a high hill. Over the SHOT comes the distant sound of ram's horns. The walls of the city are seen to crumble and fall, accompanied by a distant roar.

405.   CLOSE SHOT   GOD AND MOSES
God is watching the distant scene. The blind Moses, his eyes upward, is listening with astonishment. The sound of the falling walls comes over the SHOT. There is a pause, and from the distant conquerors comes the sound of "Joshua Fit de Battle of Jericho."

MOSES:
> You've did it, Lawd! You've tooken it! Listen to de chillun—dey's in de land of Canaan at las'! You'se de only God dey ever was, ain't you, Lawd?

406.   MED. SHOT   GOD AND MOSES
as God's arm goes around Moses's shoulder again.

GOD:

>   Come on, ol' man.

They continue up the hill, the song ending as we

FADE OUT

FADE IN

407.   INT. SUNDAY SCHOOL ROOM   CLOSE SHOT   THE SEXTON
The little boy is now sitting on his lap listening, and
Myrtle sits beside him. They are all interested in Mr.
Deshee, whose voice comes over the SHOT.

DESHEE'S VOICE:

>   But even dat scheme didn' wukk. Caize after dey got
>   into de land of Canaan dey went to de dogs ag'in.
>   An' dey went into bondage ag'in. Only dis time it
>   was in de wicked city of Babylon.

MYRTLE:

>   What dey do dat was so wicked?

DESHEE'S VOICE:

>   Oh, dey blasphemed, an' sinned against de Lawd—
>   'n' lots of things you wouldn't understan' yit. Yo'
>   gran'pa knows what I mean. It was like an' all-night
>   barrelhouse over in N'Orleans, Mr. Cluty.

Myrtle looks up at her grandfather, who nods his head
comprehendingly.

SEXTON:

>   Umm-hmmm.

DISSOLVE TO:

408.   FULL SHOT   SMOKE-FILLED NEGRO DANCE HALL-CAFE
Over the SHOT comes the music of a vigorous but not par-
ticularly talented jazz band. It is playing a jazz version of
"Go Down, Moses." Perhaps twenty small tables are oc-
cupied by parties of Negro men and women, mostly

young, in shoddy and shabby versions of conventional evening dress. The decorations are the gaudy, ugly attempts at elegance one would see in such a place. One table, conspicuous in that it will seat eight persons whereas the other tables will seat not more than four, beside the dance floor but slightly removed from the others, is unoccupied. On it is a sign, Reserved for King and Guests.[41]

409.　MED. SHOT　DANCE FLOOR
The floor is filled with dancers. The band continues.

410.　MED. CLOSE SHOT　GROUP ON FLOOR
The music continues over the SHOT. One of the male dancers, over his partner's shoulder, greets someone off scene.

DANCER:
　When did you git to Babylon, Freddie?

411.　CLOSE SHOT　ANOTHER NEGRO
exchanging the greeting. The music continues.

MAN:
　Come in on number seven yesterday. (He points to his partner.) How you like dis baby, Joe?

The girl swings around in front of CAMERA so that she can look at her escort's friend. She smiles at him.

412.　CLOSE SHOT　FIRST DANCER

DANCER:
　Hot dog! She could be de king's pet!

413.　CLOSE SHOT　ENTRANCE FROM THE FOYER INTO THE CAFE
The music comes over the scene. The head waiter-master of ceremonies is standing in the doorway looking apprehensively into the foyer.

MAN'S VOICE (off scene):
Here dey is!

MASTER OF CEREMONIES (to dancers):
Stop!

414. MED. CLOSE SHOT   THE BAND
The conductor is looking off scene. He signals the orchestra to stop, which it does.

415. MED. CLOSE SHOT   DANCE FLOOR NEAR THE MASTER OF CEREMONIES
The dancers stop.

416. CLOSE SHOT   MASTER OF CEREMONIES

MASTER OF CEREMONIES:
Tonight's guest of honor, de king of Babylon an' party of five.

417. FULL SHOT   ROOM
The dancers have all stopped and are clearing a way for the entrance of the king to his table.

418. MED. CLOSE SHOT   BAND
The conductor has his baton raised, looking off scene expectantly. Then he gives the signal and the band begins "Hail, de King of Bab-Bab-Babylon." The voices of the dancers sing the words.

419. MED. CLOSE SHOT   DOORWAY
The master of ceremonies, all smiles, is waiting expectantly. A waiter, looking behind him as he smilingly walks into the room, is followed by the king and five of the dancing girls of his court. The king wears an ill-fitting but swanky full-dress suit with white tie. Around his neck is an ornament more like a lavaliere than anything else, which hangs down over his shirt front. On his head is a woman's tiara. He also wears a long robe of some-

thing that might approximate ermine. The girls are immediately behind him, dressed in varying knee-length costumes; one of them has a hula skirt. Without stopping, the king glances over his shoulder toward the girls.

420. CLOSE TRUCKING SHOT   PRECEDING KING
who advances toward his table. The singing comes over the SHOT.

KING (looking back at girls):
    Wait till you see de swell table I got. (To one of the girls.) Come yere, newcomer.

One of the girls rushes to his side, as they continue to walk, approaching the table. The king puts his arm around the girl's waist.

421. MED. FULL SHOT   ROOM
The people are still singing. The king continues toward the table. The waiters have reached the table and are pulling out chairs. The king reaches the table and sits down. His new favorite is seated beside him. Two or three waiters stand around the table. The dancers are still standing on the dance floor.

422. CLOSE SHOT   KING AND FAVORITE
She coyly slaps his shoulder with both hands as he whispers to her.

423. FULL SHOT   ROOM
The song concludes with the shout of "Hooray!"

424. CLOSE SHOT   KING AND FAVORITE
The king acknowledges the welcome with a slight wave of the hand and again turns to the favorite.

KING:
    Remin' me to send you a peck of rubies in de mo'nin'.

425.　MED. CLOSE SHOT　KING'S TABLE
The party is now seated, and the master of ceremonies
stands before them.

MASTER OF CEREMONIES:
　　King, I want to bid you welcome on behalf of de
　　management.

KING:
　　Much obliged. How's de revelry goin'?

MASTER OF CEREMONIES:
　　De sky's de limit!

KING:
　　Good. I've invited my frien', de high priest of de He-
　　brews, to drop in later. You know what he looks like?

MASTER OF CEREMONIES:
　　No, suh, but we'll be on de lookout fo' him.

KING:
　　He looks like a gran'daddy, but he know his way
　　aroun'. (The master of ceremonies bows and leaves
　　the scene.) Okay. Now le's have a li'l good time. (To the
　　girls.) Please de king. (To the orchestra.) Let 'er go,
　　boys.

The girls leave the scene, as the music starts.

426.　FULL SHOT　THE GIRLS ON THE DANCE FLOOR
They begin to dance.

427.　CLOSE SHOT　THREE OF THE GIRLS DANCING
as the music becomes faster.

428.　CLOSE SHOT　ONE OF THE RINGSIDE TABLES
Its occupants are smiling, delighted with the dancing.

428A.　CLOSE SHOT　LEADER AND MEMBERS OF THE ORCHESTRA
at work.

429.   MED. CLOSE SHOT   NEAR KING'S TABLE
Two of the dancing girls in the foreground. The king is
excited.

KING:
    Hot fat! Dat's de way! Dey ain't nobody in de worl'
    kin squirm like de Babylon gals![42]

430.   MED. SHOT   HATCHECK COUNTER IN ENTRANCEWAY TO
CAFE
The music comes over the SHOT. The master of ceremo-
nies is leading a patriarchal old man by the arm, the CAM-
ERA TRUCKING before them. The old man is puzzled.

MASTER OF CEREMONIES:
    I'm glad I spotted you. You'd have gone right by de
    place. De king is expectin' you.

PROPHET:
    De king is expectin' me?

The prophet is puzzled and a little frightened as he mut-
ters, unheard by the master of ceremonies who is looking
off scene and holding his hand up to catch the king's
attention:

PROPHET:
    I don't know anybody yere. I wouldn't come in such
    a place.

431.   CLOSE SHOT   KING
looking off scene at the prophet.

KING:
    Stop!

432.   MED. FULL SHOT   ROOM
The dancers and the music stop. The prophet and the
master of ceremonies are now only a few feet from the
king's table.

KING:
> What's de idea, bustin' up my party?

433.   CLOSE SHOT   KING, MASTER OF CEREMONIES, AND
PROPHET

MASTER OF CEREMONIES:
> Why, yere's de high priest!

KING:
> What? Why, de high priest is a fashion plate! Dis is jes' an ol' drunk.

Two waiters join the group.

MASTER OF CEREMONIES:
> Why, of co'se! (To the waiters.) Toss dis ol' drunk out o' yere!

The waiters grab the prophet as if to take him away.

KING (to waiters):
> Wait a minute. (To the prophet.) What right you got gittin' into society? What you do fo' a livin'?

PROPHET:
> I'm a prophet of de Lawd.

KING:
> Oh, you a prophet, is you? Well, go ahead an' prophesy.

434.   CLOSE SHOT   PROPHET AND MASTER OF CEREMONIES
The prophet turns to go. The master of ceremonies stops him.

MASTER OF CEREMONIES:
> You heard de king. Go ahead!

435.   WIDER ANGLE   CENTERING ON PROPHET

PROPHET:
> Sons an' daughters of Babylon!

As he speaks, one of the dancing girls burlesques his simple gestures.

PROPHET:

> De wrath of Gawd ain' gonter be held back much longer! I'm tellin' you, repent befo' it's too late!

The other girls and people at nearby tables are laughing and giggling at the girl burlesqueing the prophet.

PROPHET:

> Repent befo' Jehovah casts down de same fire dat burned up Sodom an' Gomorrah.

436.   MED. SHOT   ENTRANCE TO CAFE

The prophet's voice comes over the SHOT.

PROPHET'S VOICE:

> You children of Israel dat's given yo'selves over to de evil ways of yo' oppressors, repent befo' de—

The high priest, with a pretty girl on his arm, enters during this speech.

HIGH PRIEST:

> Whoa, dere! (The prophet's voice stops.) What you botherin' de king fo'?

437.   MED. SHOT   GROUP

PROPHET (turning):

> An' you, de high priest of all Israel, walking de town wid de scum of de earth!

KING:

> Seems to be a frien' of yours, Jake.

HIGH PRIEST (advancing past the prophet to the king's table, the girl on his arm):

> Aw, he used to be a preacher, but I kicked 'im out of de church. He wasn't broad-minded.

The high priest is now close to the king's table. His girl is greeting the other members of the king's party.

HIGH PRIEST:
>   Don' let 'im bother you none.

The king is no longer looking at the prophet and is shaking hands with the high priest.

PROPHET:
>   You have offended our Gawd an' he's gonter smite you down jes' like he's gonter smite down all dis wicked worl'!

KING (annoyed by the prophet):
>   Wait a minute. I'm gittin' tired of dis. Don't t'row 'im out. Shoot 'im down!

438. CLOSE SHOT PROPHET

PROPHET (looking up):
>   Oh, Lawd—

There is the sound of a pistol shot. The prophet falls.

439. CLOSE SHOT MASTER OF CEREMONIES
smiling, looking off scene as he puts a revolver back in his hip pocket. He looks down at the dead prophet off scene.

MASTER OF CEREMONIES:
>   He's dead, king.[43]

440. CLOSE SHOT KING AND HIGH PRIEST
The high priest stands near the king, looking down at the prophet off scene.

HIGH PRIEST:
>   Don' know whether you should have done that, king.

KING (picking his teeth):
>   Why not?

HIGH PRIEST (a pleasing idea enters his mind):
> I don' know whether de Lawd would like it.

KING:
> Now, Jake, you know yo' Lawd ain' payin' much at-
> tention to dis man's town. (A little frightened.) It's
> tho'ly protected by de gods of Babylon.

HIGH PRIEST (his face still averted from the king):
> I know, but jes' de same—

KING (nervously):
> Look yere, s'pose I give you a couple hund'ed pieces
> of silver. Don't you s'pose you kin persuade yo' Gawd
> to keep his hands off?

HIGH PRIEST (his plan fulfilled):
> Well, of co'se we could try. (Nodding familiarly to
> the king.) I guess I kin square things up. (He puts
> his hands together prayerfully, speaks whiningly.)
> Oh, Lawd, please fo'give my ol' frien' de king of
> Babylon. (There are titters of laughter from those
> nearby.) He didn't know what he was doin'. He was
> jes'—

There is a clap of thunder, and the screen is black for a
second. Screams of terror are heard. We dim up on

441.   MED. CLOSE SHOT   NEAR KING'S TABLE
But now an intense light from a new angle in the center
of the dance floor almost blinds those present. Their faces
are frozen with terror as the CAMERA PANS from group to
group. God's voice comes over the SHOT.

GOD'S VOICE (in tones of doom):
> Dat's about enough. I'se stood all I kin from you. I
> tried to make dis a good earth. I helped Adam, I
> helped Noah, I helped Moses, an' I helped David.
> What's de grain dat grew out of de seed? Sin! Nothin'
> but sin throughout de whole worl'. I've given you
> ev'y chance. I sent you warriors an' prophets. I've

given you laws an' commandments, an' you betrayed
my trust. Ev'ything I've given you, you've defiled.
Ev'y time I've fo'given you, you've mocked me. An'
now de high priest of Israel tries to trifle wid my
name. Listen, you chillun of darkness, yo' Lawd is
tired.

The music of the choir singing "Death's Gwineter Lay His
Cold Icy Hands on Me" also comes over the SHOT, at first
softly. CAMERA CONTINUES TO PAN.

GOD'S VOICE:
I'm tired of de struggle to make you worthy of de
breath I gave you. I put you in bondage ag'in to save
you an' yo' worse dan you was amongst de fleshpots
of Egypt. So I renounce you.

442.   CLOSE SHOT   GOD   CAMERA POINTING UP TO GOD'S BACK
Both his hands are raised in the air.

GOD:
Listen to de words of yo' Lawd God Jehovah, for dey
is de las' words yo' ever hear from me. I repent of
dese people dat I have made an' I will deliver dem no
more.

The light starts to fade, and the wailing high note in the
chorus of the choir coincides with the groans of the
Babylonians, as we

SLOWLY FADE OUT

FADE IN
443.   INT. GOD'S OFFICE   MED. CLOSE SHOT   DAY
The sound of the choir singing "You Hear de Lambs A-
Cryin'" comes over the SHOT. God is seated at his desk,
facing the CAMERA. Over God's shoulder we see Gabriel
enter the room.

GOD (wearily):
Who is it?

GABRIEL:
> De delegation, Lawd.

GOD (with a sigh of patient resignation):
> Tell 'em to come in.

444. CLOSE SHOT   DOORWAY
Song continues. Gabriel turns toward the doorway and nods. In answer to his signal Abraham, Isaac, Jacob, and Moses enter.

GOD'S VOICE:
> Good mo'nin', gen'lemen.

ABRAHAM, ISAAC, JACOB, AND MOSES:
> Good mo'nin', Lawd.

GOD'S VOICE:
> What kin I do fo' you?

MOSES:
> You know, Lawd. Go back to our people.

445. MED. CLOSE SHOT   GOD   FROM MOSES'S ANGLE
Song continues.

GOD (swinging around from his desk):
> Ev'y day fo' hund'eds of years you boys have come in to ask dat same thing. De answer is still de same. I repented of de people I made, an' would deliver dem no more. Good mo'nin', gen'lemen.

446. CLOSE SHOT   THE FOUR VISITORS
The song continues.

ABRAHAM, ISAAC, JACOB, AND MOSES (rising):
> Good mo'nin', Lawd.

They file out of the office. The song ends.

447. FULL SHOT   OFFICE
God, who has risen, slowly goes to the window.

GOD:

> Gabe, why do dey do it?

GABRIEL:

> I 'spect dey think you gonter change yo' min'.

GOD:

> Dey don' know me. (He looks down toward the earth.) An' you don' know me down dere, either!

448–53. OMITTED[44]

454.   MED SHOT   GOD AND GABRIEL

GABRIEL:

> What dey doin' now, Lawd?

GOD:

> It's a man. He ain't exactly prayin'. But he's talkin' in such a way I got to listen. (He looks up as though he were listening to the voice.) His name is—Hezdrel. He's a man no one ever heard of. . . . I kin heah his voice now.[45]

GABRIEL:

> Den tell it to stop.

GOD (smiling sadly):

> I fin' I don' want to do dat, either. Dey's gittin' ready to take Jerusalem down dere. Dat was my big fine city. Dis Hezdrel, he's jes' one of de defenders. (He puts his hands over his ears.) I ain' comin' down. You hear me? I ain' comin' down! (He looks at Gabriel.) Go ahead, Gabriel. 'Tend to yo' chores. I'm gonter keep wukkin' heah.

455.   CLOSE-UP   GABRIEL

GABRIEL:

> I hates to see you feelin' like dis, Lawd.

[456–61.] CLOSE SHOT   GOD   FROM A SIDE VIEW
as he leans out the window.

GOD:
> I hear you. I know yo' fightin' bravely, but I told you
> I ain't comin' down.[46]

462.   CLOSE SHOT   HEZDREL
A group of four soldiers enters the scene. Three rush past
Hezdrel and out of the SHOT. The fourth speaks to Hezdrel.

SOLDIER:
> De fightin's stopped fo' de night, Hezdrel. Dey gon-
> ter begin ag'in at cockcrow. King Herod say he's
> gonter take de temple tomorrow, burn de ark of de
> covenant, an' put us to de sword.

HEZDREL:
> You ready, ain't you?

SOLDIER:
> Yes, Hezdrel.

HEZDREL:
> Good. Take dese yere wounded men wid you an' git
> 'em took care of. (Musingly.) So King Herod's gonna
> burn de temple, is he? Well, what if dey do? If dey
> kill us we'll jes' leap out of our skins, right into de
> lap of God. De Lawd'll be yere, lookin' out fo' his
> people as usual.

462A.   CLOSE SHOT   GOD AT WINDOW

GOD:
> Why don' you leave me alone? You know you ain'
> talkin' to me. (Almost pleadingly.) Is you talkin' to
> me? (He listens to the unheard voice.) I cain' stan' yo'
> talkin' dat way. I kin only hear part of what you
> sayin', an' it puzzles me. (Loudly.) Don' you know
> you cain't puzzle God? (He is now completely de-
> feated; then, tenderly, as if speaking to a very small

ries of "Le's go, Hezdrel!"

, boys!

men, the CAMERA TRUCKS BEFORE
s to sing "March On."

HEZDREL AND SOLDIERS
head, their faces grimly set, as they
g modulates through the following
tempo of "Rise, Shine, Give God de

DISSOLVE TO:

SH FRY IN HEAVEN
choir comes over the SHOT. The illu-
l tones darker than that of the first fish
oir is marching more slowly, and the
rs are standing in quiet groups about
g God, who is sitting in an armchair in
the CAMERA. Gabriel is at his side. The
P TO A

D AND GABRIEL

little pensive, Lawd. (God nods his head
he is deep in his thoughts.) Want a seegar,

ng at Gabriel):
, Gabriel.

erly):
awful pensive, Lawd. You been sittin' yere,
is way an awful long time. Is it somethin'
Lawd?

ious, Gabriel.

---

child.) You want me to come down dere *ve'y* much? You know I said I wouldn't come down. (He looks about; loudly.) Why don' he answer me a little? (Then with a completely bogus dignity, having been thoroughly routed.) Listen! I'll tell you what I'll do. I ain' gonter promise you nothin', an I ain't gonter do nothin' to help you. I'm jes' feelin' a little low, an' I'm only comin' down to make myself feel a little better, dat's all.

He turns and walks out the door, CAMERA PANNING WITH HIM.

463.   MED. SHOT   SOLDIERS
picking up wounded.

464.   CLOSE SHOT   HEZDREL
The firelight is flickering over his face.

HEZDREL (musingly):
So dey gonter take de temple in de mo'nin'. (He glances up off scene at the temple.) We'll be waitin' for 'em. Jes' remember, boys, when dey kill us we leap out of our skins, right into de lap of God.

A light which does not illuminate the background, but glows about Hezdrel's face, is apparent. The campfire light is no longer noticeable. Hezdrel senses something strange and looks about him. He sees God standing nearby.

465.   CLOSE SHOT   HEZDREL AND GOD

GOD:
Hello, Hezdrel—Adam.

HEZDREL:
Who is you?

GOD:
I's an ol' preacher from back in de hills. I jes' got yere. Yo' boys is fightin' bravely, ain't you?

HEZDREL:

> We may be killed, but we ain't skeered.

God shows he's pleased.

GOD:

> Why is you so brave?

HEZDREL:

> Caize, we got faith.

GOD:

> Faith? In who?

HEZDREL:

> In our dear Lawd God.

GOD:

> But didn't he desert you?

HEZDREL:

> Not de God we trust in.

GOD:

> Who's he?

HEZDREL:

> De God of mercy.

GOD (terrified):

> But ain't dey only one God?

HEZDREL:

> I don't know. But ol' preacher Hosea say not to be skeered of God. Caize he ain't a God of wrath and vengeance no more.

GOD:

> Where'd Hosea ever hear about mercy?

HEZDREL:

> I guess he found it the same way I found it, the only way anyone can find it.

GABRIEL:

> Lawd, is de time come fo' me to blow?

GOD:

> Not yet, Gabriel. I'm jes' thinkin'.[49]

Gabriel raises his hand.

471.   MED. CLOSE SHOT   THE CHOIR AND LEADER

The leader motions to the choir. They stop their singing and marching.

472.   CLOSE SHOT   GOD AND GABRIEL

GABRIEL:

> What about, Lawd?

GOD:

> Somethin' de boy Hezdrel tol' me, 'bout Hosea an' himself. How dey found mercy. Mercy. (He thinks hard.) Through sufferin', he said.

GABRIEL (in a whisper):

> Yes, Lawd.

GOD:

> I'm tryin' to find it, too. It's awful impo'tant, Gabriel, to all de people on my earth.

473.   CLOSE-UP   GOD

There is agony on his face as a new thought strikes him.

GOD:

> Did he mean dat even God must suffer? Listen! Dere's someone else on de earth.

A MAN'S VOICE:

> Oh, look at him! Dey gonter make him carry it up dat high hill! Dey gonter nail him to it! Oh, dat's a terrible burden fo' one man to carry!

The CAMERA STARTS TO PULL BACK as God rises from his chair.

GOD (murmuring softly):
  Yes.

The choir bursts fortissimo into "Hallelujah, King Jesus." God's head slowly turns.

474.   FULL SHOT   COMPANY   AS SEEN THROUGH GOD'S EYES
The CAMERA PANS over the entire company. The sun comes out again, and heaven is radiant. The choir forms part of an immense semicircle of the hosts of heaven, all facing God. All are singing.

475.   CLOSE SHOT   GOD
smiling. The clouds start to form in front of him. The music continues over the following

                                          DISSOLVE TO:

476.   INT. CORNER SUNDAY SCHOOL   CLOSE SHOT   SEXTON,
MYRTLE, AND THE LITTLE BOY
The music continues softly over the SHOT. The little boy is asleep in his grandfather's arms, his head against the old man's shoulder. Myrtle is smiling faintly, as if in a reverie. The tips of the sexton's fingers meet and part, and meet again. He, too, is speculating.

                                          FADE OUT

THE END

Annotation to the Screenplay

1 Like so many stage plays, *The Green Pastures* required considerable opening up of the action through means of cinematic devices. As late as the final draft of the script, Marc Connelly had still not settled on a format for the main titles. At first the titles were intended to be seen as a result of clouds being pushed aside by cleaning women in God's office. Down in a corner of the screen a mortal child is inexplicably watching, thereby breaking the suspension of belief necessary to the success of a fantasy. The letters were to be seen as great metallic things being polished and dusted. As the titles faded, the music was to diminish and segue into a single churchbell pealing in a miniature exterior of a country church through which we were to dissolve to a small corner where we see a sexton and a boy meant to introduce us to the plain rural folk and their spiritual life.

Instead, in the release print the credits opened as parchment pages of an antique book reposing beside a lighted candle. At the end of the titles, a celestial "crawl" introduces the film with a "Foreword" that had not appeared in earlier versions:

God appears in many forms to those who believe in Him. Thousands of Negroes in the Deep South visualize God and Heaven in terms of people and things they know in their everyday life. *The Green Pastures* is an attempt to portray that humble reverent conception.

Fade to black and then up on the church setting.

2 Throughout the film, Connelly and his associates tightened the action, visualized verbal description, and trimmed dialogue, scenes, and "business," sometimes apparently spontaneously, a process that resulted in a neatly economical film that suffered only at the end from constriction that blurred God's motives.

3 Throughout, the dialogue is tinged with what seem to be actors' spontaneous embellishments and refinements of sounds assimilated by Connelly's ear. In the film, the sexton says "li'l chillun," "dis watch," and various ejaculations not precisely in keeping with the script. Similarly, bits of business such as holding the watch to his ear with eyes tilted heavenward were either left to the actors or emerged from daily direction on the set.

The sexton's recounting of the uses of his watch while calling the faithful to prayer (see figure 1) was one of several establishing sequences that sketched in the anatomy of rural southern black life. The scenes were added to the play script as though movie audiences were less knowledgeable than theater audiences.

4 Most substantive changes between stage and screen dialogue merely refined rhetorical devices. Here, the remonstration "wouldn't do you no harm to go back to Sunday school too" became more sharply focused on the action: "Dat's [idle guitar strumming] goin' to break yo' min' [mind] down."

Sometimes, Connelly's overstated descriptions of costuming were modulated in the development from page to screen. Here, the young girl is "flashily" dressed; on the screen she appears in a trim skirt, only slightly too short, with gingham-accented collar and apron, set off by new high-heeled shoes. If anything, she would be underdressed for a black church service.

5 Connelly appeared to perceive sin as a kind of archetypical Harlem street scene evil, but this view was, in the final draft, considerably tightened and focused only where it appeared relevant as, for example, before the deluge. Here, the antics of three roustabouts are cut so as to fix attention on Mr. Deshee's virtuous life, thus allowing the depiction of rakehells and wastrels to be deferred until they can be used as symbols of the pervasive, universal sin that was to be cleansed by the symbolic event of the flood.

6 Some rhetorical tightening was simply in the interests of economy. Here, a lengthier phrase from the play becomes merely a cryptic "maybe so."

7 Some cinematic devices, especially atmospheric touches, appear on film but not on the page. Here, as Deshee and Carlisle walk into the frame (itself an entrance that survived from stage technique), a man mounted on a mule passes through the background as though to point up the rural setting with greater precision.

8 Twenty-three scenes into the script we arrive at last at the opening of the Broadway play, the recounting of Genesis in Deshee's Sunday school. Thenceforward, cinematic devices begin to intrude, as, for example, when the schoolroom that provides the basis in reality from which we shall depart into theological fantasy begins to differentiate among the characters of the children by cutting to winsome close-ups as they raise theological points. Two years earlier, DuBose Heyward, the author of *Porgy*, wrote a Harlem prologue to Eugene O'Neill's *The*

Emperor Jones as a cinematic means of placing Jones in a plausible black setting from which we may watch his rise to power. Connelly uses this sequence in much the same way as a filmic prologue that made use of the practice of "establishing shots," or introductory shots, usually broadly encompassing, that place the viewer in a social milieu and a physical environment.

9 Such stage directions are given filmic values by varying shots from wide to close-up with varying points of view, all emerging out of a master shot from the point of view of the dramatist's "fourth wall." In routine film style, perhaps influenced by the experienced co-director William Keighley, staginess is avoided by cutting from close-up to close-up on the reading of a line or a bit of business. Consequently, *The Green Pastures* deviated from theatrical practice but achieved no more than prosaic cinematic values.

10 Fred Jackman's storm described here was excised, perhaps to postpone the introduction of the supernatural so as to establish a firm foundation in the secular world.

11 The transition from script to screen generated a certain subsurface tension between the media at this point. The descriptions of heaven have been shortened and generally left to the imagination of cinematographer Jackman's ingenuity. Connelly's racial descriptions are saved from embarrassing racial connotations by the process of filming. His "two buck angels" become merely two men dressed in angelic mufti. An occasional bit is garbled in translation. Here a cherub in the film cries, "Ah's an Innian [Indian]." In the script he is described as an Indian but has no line to read.

12 The heavenly montage is brought back to the human scale by means of a series of medium close-ups and by bits of business perhaps inspired on the set. "You sho' got pretty wings," a woman angel says to her male companion whose wings she delicately strokes. "Dey's jes' mah ol' ones," he replies with humility. (The insertion of these montage shots apparently replaced scenes 31–33. The elision of scene numbers elsewhere in the screenplay usually indicates irregularities in numbering caused by revisions and changed pages.)

13 The debate over the merits of minnows and worms is one of several exchanges between men and women excised with the result that an intense, bitter edginess between nagging black women and casual black males is considerably muted. Thus a strong note of intersexual warfare is dampened and replaced by having the women turn their sharp tongues on the endearingly misbehaving children.

14 The theological definition of the nature of evil and of Satan is cut here, perhaps because in the logic of the situation Satan might be appropriately white, thereby disqualifying the film from seeking a small-town, nationwide, "crossover" audience of blacks and whites.

15 Scenes 42 and 58, an absurdly false and extraneous sequence, are cut. They dramatized the handing out of Sunday school "cyards [cards]," a sort of diploma, to the kids whose names were intended to be patently "colored." Among the elided names were Gineeva Chaproe and Nootzie Winebush. Connelly had hit upon, but failed to catch the spirit of, the Negro practice of inventing given names to go with commonplace surnames, such as Jones or Smith, to create an interesting metrical effect.

16 A line is added here to provide motivation for the spanking. "Yeah, but he's playin' too rough!" The child's "squeal" of delight is eliminated. Presumably, spanking in heaven is permitted as a reasonable weapon of the authorities, much as it might have been in the arsenal of poor harassed secular parents.

17 Boiled custard appears in cooking literature in several forms. Like most foods, each of the dishes can stand for the communal fellowship evoked by a church picnic or fish fry, but one variant may hold a special meaning related to the church's role as a restorative of spirits worn out with the grind of secular life. Boiled custard is unique by definition because most custards are baked after they are boiled so as to impart firmness and a good brown coloring. See, for example, Jim Harwood and Ed Callahan, *Soul Food Cookbook* (San Francisco: Nitty Gritty Productions, 1969), p. 202, in which the milk, sugar, butter, and other ingredients are boiled not at all but put immediately in the oven. In Fannie Merritt Farmer's *Boston Cooking-School Cook Book*, 7th ed. (Boston: Little Brown, 1942), pp. 510–11, the custard itself is not boiled but merely heated over a double boiler for seven minutes, and then either browned in the oven or chilled in order to give it the firmness that will allow eating with a spoon. This method is also found in two versions in a recent edition of a book compiled by Mrs. Simon Kander of Milwaukee, in 1901, *The New Settlement Cook Book*, 20th ed. (New York: Simon and Schuster, 1954). It is in Mrs. M. E. Porter's *New Southern Cookery Book* (Philadelphia: John E. Potter and Company, 1871; facsimile edition, New York: Promontory Press, 1974), pp. 414–15, that we find a recipe that might be the source of the special feelings that the heavenly black picnickers have toward "b'iled custud." Mrs. Porter lists her recipe under "cookery for the sick." In other

words, the dish is associated with nurture, restoration of lost powers, recovery from the pain of the secular world. And it is simply, even hastily, tossed together in a teacup and perhaps poured over a bit of toast with a little grated nutmeg.

18 Here, firmament is intended as a Negro malapropism by punning the word from ecclesiastical Latin with "ferment" and then extending its meaning, as Genesis does, to mean the firmness of the newly minted earth. It seems more recognizable than it is effective as humor.

19 The singularity and the integrity of God are established through the use of frequent one-shot close-ups from a tilted-up angle that conveys a sense of majesty. Mere mortals and angels tend to appear in groups and two-shots in medium close-ups, perhaps a legacy of stage blocking as much as a conscious device of Hollywood movie makers.

20 Many sound and music effects are considerably diminished from Connelly's expectations, as here where no effects at all are used.

21 The inappropriately testy remonstrances by the females in scenes 86 and 87 were cut, thus preserving a reverent mood and saving the audience from a repetition of the reference to "firmament."

22 As though to give God his due, he is seen in close-up here with an added line: "Ah jes' made a garden too." In scene 98, in order to give him a day of rest, he adds: "I'll be back Saddy [Saturday]."

23 Scenes 99 through 117 represent the opposite strategy prevalent in the rest of the film, in that Connelly abandoned a series of intricate process shots in favor of a few special effects in the form of a thundering chiaroscuro storm sequence. God enters the earth by taking a stroll down a misty hill. Adam's entrance is as simple: we see him fully rounded and flexing his newly fashioned muscles, standing upright, rather than prone as the script prescribes, and paying homage to God who stands nearby in his frock coat, admiring his handiwork. Jackman's ingenuity was tested only in the process shots of Adam and God conversing (Rex Ingram played both) and those in which Eve materializes out of the air. God's charging them with their mutual duties has the ring of a marriage ceremony, as though to appease the censors.

24 Once again, at the last moment Connelly chose to depict sin as the subject of God's sermons rather than as a dramatization. When Cain kills, for example, God's ambiguous line is cut: "Well, I ain't sayin' you right an' I ain't sayin' you wrong." In its place, God exiles Cain: "Yo' better git yo'self down de road an' far away." Having established the nature of sin, Connelly then cut an entire sequence in the land of

Nod in which sin was to be symbolized in the person of Cain's girl played as a shameless hussy (scenes 133–39). Once again, Connelly had avoided depicting black urban street life as sinful.

25 God's office as shot was spare and considerably less cluttered—lacking the hat rack, framed oleograph, cuspidor, and obtrusive sound effects sketched in the script—thus allowing Connelly to achieve his original intention of granting God a quiet dignity.

26 God's return to earth in scenes 139–78 is largely a filmed play with few changes. The apocryphal Zeba is an example of the minimal tinkering: in the play she is a "wanton," in the film a "chippie." The narrative is told in wide establishing shots intercut with composed, stage-blocked clusters of characters. Even God gets few close-ups, perhaps suggesting a decline in faith. Only the startling intrusion of Cain the Sixth and his "gal," Zeba, seen from God's point of view foreshadows the eventual depiction of sin as the bugbears of the Negro middle class—dancing, drinking, gambling, overdressing.

27 In the gambling sequence, scenes 185–201, Connelly passed up an opportunity to dramatize the failings of the derelict mothers of riff-raff. While adopting the point of view of "respectable" parents—that close supervision saves children from a life of sin—Connelly cut considerable detail from the indictment by allowing the young crap-shooter's mother to be characterized by the single detail of having deserted her family for a railroad man. The audience knew by his positive images the virtuous life; he seemed to wish to avoid the charge of racial stereotyping that might follow from a too vivid account of black sin. Some black critics made the charge anyway.

28 God has seen man in the round and is not pleased. As God walks the earth, sin is rife, yet here too Connelly will not be drawn into an originally intended mauve depiction of black sin. In the sequence following scene 201, God's return to secular life as written was larded with scenes of erotic and sensual wantonness. On the screen, perhaps to mollify Hollywood's self-imposed censor or hoped-for black bourgeois audiences, the viewer observes sin in a considerably softened, somewhat remote truck shot that moves with God as he strides through the scene. The effect approximates that of a broad, colorful Brueghel painting that induces a mellow view of human foibles as opposed to, say, a more close-up, darkly corrupt Hogarth etching of London's poor rabble. Dialogue sequences reporting on details of thievery, drunkenness, and rascality are slashed in great chunks from earlier drafts. In a typical bit in scenes 207–15, a flashily dressed woman, upon learning that her neglected children are "gonna rob a grocery

store" and "pick pockets," warns them with cool parental firmness: "Don't git arrested." Clearly, the sequence would have removed Connelly from his tacit alliance with middle-class respectables because the incident departed from the notion that parental neglect caused crime and instead offered a parent as the supervisor of crime.

29 Noah's long sequence marks the high moment of the dominance of cinematic over dramatic devices. As God meets Noah, a long, wrathful speech justifying the impending deluge is cut as though the visual impact of the flood itself will carry the burden of the message. From scene 219 onward, details of Noah's domestic life are boiled down, including an extraneous bit about incest, perhaps in deference to Eddie Anderson's star status as well as cinematic considerations. A polite introduction of his clearly middle-class respectable wife becomes merely, "Dis mah ole lady."

30 The theological motive for the deluge is distilled from the dramatic version down to a joint statement of Noah's decent respectability, which allows him a parole from the effects of God's wrath. Here as elsewhere throughout the film, the music track is considerably less imposing than intended, as though the combination of visual and aural effects would overload the audience's sensory circuits.

31 Probably in the interests of cinematic economy, sequences depicting Noah's sons (Shem, Ham, and Japheth) were cut, thereby restoring the original structure and scale of scene 9 in the Broadway play.

32 The darkling sky, the beginning of the rain, the last hysterical loading of the ark, the shrill hazing by the sinful onlookers are here built into a powerfully wrought visual climax that could not have been possible on the stage. To make room for the sequence, Connelly reduced the badinage, ad libs, reaction shots, snippets of expository dialogue, Mrs. Noah's scenes, gags about the ark's inadequacies, and passages in which Noah is hazed (he is dropped from the rolls of the local burial society and jeered as "ol' Manatee"). Many of the cuts may have been made as late as the final editing, perhaps in keeping with Hollywood wisdom that dictated keeping expensively mounted shots in the final cut whenever possible so that "every dollar can be seen on the screen." The sales executives most certainly would have argued for retaining the sequences most heavily laden with special effects and costly sets. Indeed, it could be argued that scenes 278–82, in which the loading of the ark unfolds, were written purely for their cinematic and box-office impact.

By way of contrast, the scenes of the flood waters at crest and then receding, the releasing of the dove, and the descent of God to the deck of the ark seem prosaic and cheaply done, as though in the previous scenes Connelly and Jackman had reached the limits of Warner Brothers' budget and patience. This is not to say these anticlimactic scenes fail. To make room for the visual augmentation of the deluge sequence, considerable material meant to give depth to background figures was sacrificed, resulting in better pacing, sense of direction, and simpler line of plot. In keeping with their reduced scale in earlier scenes, Noah's strong-willed wife and dutiful, pipe-smoking sons become no more than background furniture. Having already exploited the visual strength of the scenes in which the ark is stocked, the final cut made do without an elaborate debarking scene.

Unfortunately, in the process of tightening here, Connelly and Jackman threw away an opportunity to present a sweeping cinematic view of the new earth. Instead, the visual impression is of a cheap "tank shot." The resulting small-scale vision may have undermined the theological message of the deluge. The grand statement of monotheism, the sense of God engaged in the affairs of man, the joy of rebirth, the sources of baptism ritual in water symbolism, the hope for renewal at the heart of Christian theology are all diminished by the small scale of the frame. Thus, the whole reason "why," as God says in the play, "I feel so solemn an' serious at dis partiklar time" is lost on the audience, or at least reduced in its awesomeness. In the movie, God can only say lamely "I only hope it's goin' to wukk out all right." To explain the muddied message to the audience, Connelly inserted a new and unsuccessful scene in Deshee's Sunday school (scene 297).

In this sequence, Connelly wisely removed his strongest reference to Negro drunkenness. Before the deluge, God and Noah in a comic bit had debated the number of "kags" of "medicinal" spirits to be taken on board. In a scene perhaps intended to reveal God's wisdom in this matter, he remonstrates with Noah and forgives him his human frailty that had been revealed on the forty days at sea. Noah had grown into a hard-drinking, cussing martinet, for which God forgives him: "I don' even min' you cussin' an' drinkin'. I figure a steamboat cap'n on a long trip like you had has a right to a little redeye, jest so he don' go crazy." Black critics had already taken the stage play to task for its references to Negro drinking, so Connelly may have saved the movie from hostile black criticism.

33 In scenes 298–314, God has turned sour on mankind and impotently vents his wrath by hurling thunderbolts at the earthlings who have resumed their sinful ways. Here too, the carefully worked theology of

the drama is foreshortened and motivation weakened. God receives Abraham, Isaac, and Jacob, the Hebrew sages who help him resolve to save the Israelites from bondage in Egypt and send them to their Zion in Canaan, but the motivating lines from the play are missing, and with them the whole reason for the historic Afro-American affinity for and identification with Old Testament Jewish lore.

In the play God announces: "Seein' dat you human bein's cain't 'preciate anythin' lessen you fust wukk to git it and den keep strugglin' to hold it," thus providing the motive for requiring the Israelites to trek through the desert before reaching their promised land. The legend also gives meaning to the black experience in North America as a march from slavery to freedom, a metaphor used by generations of black preachers and political leaders as an inspiration for black activism. In the movie, Connelly throws away the point by reducing God's message to a purely personal and even flippant scale that does an injustice to the scene. "You is about de three best boys . . . dat's come up yeah since I made little apples," he says.

34 God comes to Moses unheralded, overawes him with heavenly glory, and calls upon him to lead the Israelite host out of Egypt. The scene has a quiet conviction that needs no embellishment. So scenes 321–24, played between Moses and his Midianite wife, Zipporah, become expendable despite their survival in every earlier version.

35 Moses and Aaron are introduced with greater effect in the film. In earlier versions they are either lost in the crowd or the scene opens on the rod transformed into the serpent—both versions lacking conviction because the focus of the action was either lacking or misplaced.

36 The considerable footage allotted to special effects and the visualizing scenes only sketched on the stage required the excision of biblical plagues of gnats and flies as well as a sharp exchange between Moses and Pharaoh.

37 Like the deluge sequence, the scenes played in Pharaoh's throne room grew in visual strength on film. Indeed, in its way the scene was the "blackest" in the movie. By way of comparison, the heavenly fish fry, save for dialect and a few regionalisms, could have as easily been a white picnic. But Pharaoh's court personified a Negro lodge hall, hung with ceremonial banners described by Connelly in loving detail in previous scripts.

Cinematically, the scene proved the most awkward to play; from stage to screen Connelly tried several versions, none of which made a vivid statement. In the play, the scene opens on a bored monarch waited upon by a candidate-magician. An early draft of the script begins with a tight close-up of the rod of Moses and Aaron as it changes into a serpent, and then pulls back to reveal the lodge hall. In the final script, Pharaoh barges into the crowded court to the accompaniment of music and obeisances, then turns his attention not to the tricksters but to the cruelties he has called down upon the Hebrews. None of the openings seemed to catch the balance among imposing Egyptian ceremony, humble Hebrew farmers bearing the power of their tribal god in their shepherd's rod, and the prize for which they contended—the future of the Hebrew people.

As filmed, Connelly returned to the original concept, augmented by the attributes of the camera and cutting room. He brings the viewer into the court by means of a close-up of the lodge banners with a raucous jazz theme on the sound track, thus paradoxically using a close-up as an establishing shot. Skirting along the edge of parody—he might have slipped over into white man's satire of black middle-class life in the manner of the then popular radio show *Amos 'n' Andy*—Connelly used a source of power within black communities as a symbol of the awesome power that Pharaoh must have held over the Israelites. Pharaoh in *his* court is seen in as many tilted-up close-ups as God is in *his* court. As the scene is developed visually, Pharaoh in the course of the several drafts loses a considerable number of his lines that had been used to establish the extent of his power on the stage.

38 Throughout the film, the Hall Johnson Choir dominates the sound track with a shrewdly selected repertoire of traditional Negro music. But like most dramatic uses of music before Rodgers and Hammerstein's *Oklahoma!*, the songs were ancillary to the "book," punctuating the drama rather than carrying it.

In one of the exceptions, when Moses and Aaron leave Pharaoh's court to take up the leadership of the trek to Zion, the music serves as the cutter's vehicle for carrying the viewer from the interior to the column of Israelites stretching into the desert like Eisenstein's column of pilgrims in the snow in *Alexander Nevsky*. The Negro traditional song "Go Down, Moses" carries the action under Connelly's tight direction (in the script he specified the voice he wanted to accompany certain shots and the line on which he wanted to cut). A close truck shot of marching feet is underlined by the choir on the line "let my people go." Each new shot of ever more dusty feet, ending with a sweeping crane shot of the column stretching into the desert, derived strength from a chorus of a Negro spiritual such as "I'm No Ways Weary" or "Mary, Don't You Weep." Thus black traditional music carried the narrative of Exodus, thereby making understandable to white audiences the Negro identification with Jewish history.

39 The end of the trek in the shadow of the walls of Jericho, like other sequences that held out the promise of exciting cinematic treatment, failed to live up to its potential. Joshua is introduced in bland fashion, and the battle of Jericho itself takes place off camera as a distant rumbling and a few muted trumpets.

40 Here, God and Moses should see each other as master and servant, perhaps drawn closer together by adversity, so that Moses might observe that God has begun to temper wrath with mercy. In the play, God explains to Moses why he may see heaven but not be allowed to reach Canaan: "Moses, you been a good man. You been a good leader of my people. Moses, you got me angry once, dat's true. And when you anger me, I'm a god of wrath." But the movie abandons the point. All we know is a theologically empty half-truth: "You been a good man. Now you gonter have your *own* Promised Land." The biblical concept of a "chosen people" seems thoughtlessly trimmed, thus removing the very reason why blacks derived spiritual comfort from the Old Testament.

41 Here, as elsewhere, jazz is the idiom of the urban, modern, fallen Negro while spirituals express the integrity of rural Negro culture. Unfortunately, archetype may easily segue into stereotype, and the musical metaphor sometimes makes an apparent distinction between rural "good Negroes" and urban "bad niggers." Historians have in recent years argued that the urban migration was a demoralizing experience for Afro-Americans and that urban economic depression destroyed the lower-class black family after generations of slavery could not. Nevertheless, insensitive hands have readily shaped this historical data into a Yang-and-Yin vision of black life in which humble folk Negroes who know their places are preferred over uppity, flashy, erotic, violence-prone city Negroes. Indeed, urban blacks themselves have sometimes made such a distinction between respectables and riffraff. The modern secular temper and its spoliation of traditional values has been a powerful dilemma for black clerics because black life has provided its own evocative metaphor—the migration of tradition-directed rural black folk from southern farms to the moral ambiguity of big city life. Ancient Babylon has its simile in Harlem.

42 In the Babylonian sequence, two gratuitous references to Jews that might be taken as anti-Semitic did not survive the final cut, perhaps at the behest of Hollywood censors. "Any Jew boys here?" the king asks of his courtiers. Later, he exults over the work of a few nightclub

hoofers: "Hot damn! Da's de way! Let de Jew boys see our gals kin dance better'n dere's." In the final draft he says only: "Hot fat! Dat's de way! Dey ain't nobody in de worl' kin squirm like de Babylon gals! "

43 The strength and meaning of this scene are lost because it is not clear that the old prophet is intended as a symbol of tradition that had been usurped by the flashy modernist priests who owe their status to pleasing the king. The shooting seems merely gratuitous and pointless, except as an occasion for God to raise his voice.

44 A central theological point is thrown away here. From scene 443 onward, the film departs from the play in its treatment of Hosea, the prophet who foreshadowed the New Testament concept of a merciful god. Scenes 448–53, in which the moviegoer was to perceive the growing influence of Hosea on Hebrew theology, are dropped in their entirety. Once again, an important reason for the affinity between Jewish and black Baptist theology is tossed aside in the interest of pacing or economy.

45 Connelly, having diminished the stature of Hosea, invented his own apocryphal character, Hezdrel, to serve as a bridge between Old Testament godly wrath and New Testament salvationism. Hezdrel is a kind of black Everyman, or as God puts it, "He's a man no one ever heard of," who is the first black figure to speak and act as a warrior fighting not in a holy cause but in the name of the group.

46 Beginning with scene 456, the theology of *The Green Pastures* seems all at sea. Without Hosea to prophesy the coming of a merciful god, the film at a crucial point loses conviction. God seems merely irresponsible and self-pitying. "Even bein' God ain't no bed of roses," he complains. Without Hosea's concept of a changing deity, God becomes paralyzed and remote from man's concerns. In the ten or so scenes leading up to Hezdrel's battle (scene 465) with the enemies of the Hebrew people, Connelly tried unsuccessfully to incorporate the theological trend toward a merciful god into a debate between Hezdrel and God. But some of the unfocused and incomplete dialogue, which was probably hastily drafted, was not included in the shooting script until March, less than three months before the release date. At last, Connelly chose to shoot the scene in considerably foreshortened form as a simple (and apocryphal) meeting between God and Hezdrel only moments before the battle that begins with scene 465. The script-doctoring helped make an effective scene while doing little to advance the still undeveloped theological underpinning of the movie.

47 Following scene 465, Connelly tries again to introduce Hosea but

soon abandons the idea in favor of resting the burden of the changing nature of God upon the shoulders of Hezdrel. Through his prayers he seems to take God by the hand and introduce him to the modern temper. As though Connelly had not made up his mind even as the company began shooting, he has God seek out Hezdrel. "I come a long ways to ask you somethin'," he says with ungodly humility, seeking after the sources of Hezdrel's faith in the future.

In early drafts, Connelly has Hezdrel trace his faith to "de God of Hosea," but let it drop by the time they had reached the final cut. In the film, before Hezdrel can take up Hosea's notion of a merciful god, the battle resumes and we still know too little.

48 Hezdrel's defense of Jerusalem here is more powerful than it deserves to be, indeed, is powerful at the expense of the more important matter of budding Christian salvationism that formed the core of theology that most attracted the black faithful. Nevertheless, combat provided a powerful symbol of a modern black temperament and an allegorical call to arms to defend the race's secular interests. In its way, it repeated a challenge that black younger generations often used against older preachers who placed too much unalloyed faith in salvationism.

The audience never learns the outcome of Hezdrel's battle. To fight the good fight is enough, the film seems to say. But he has planted the germ of the idea of personal salvation.

49 In the end, *The Green Pastures* retained and even accentuated its most dramaturgically disturbing structural element of the stage production. Connelly took only two and one half pages to carry God from his tribal origins to a more universal salvationism, resulting in an unfulfilled catharsis and a tacked-on ending. In the last scene, God seems out of sorts and heaven clouded by a nameless malaise. Can it be that even God must suffer in order to learn faith, a considerably daunted God asks himself. Suddenly, in the manner of an ancient deus ex machina, an angel looks over the side of heaven and, uncomprehending, sees a man bearing a cross. In a flash God learns that, indeed, God must suffer. Too hastily, the heavenly host sings "Hallelujah, King Jesus," bringing to a close the Old Testament and fulfilling Hosea's prophesy for an audience that has been denied access to all but surface motives for the action.

Production Credits

Directed by	Marc Connelly and William Keighley
Screenplay by	Marc Connelly
Choral Music Arranged and Conducted by	Hall Johnson with the Hall Johnson Choir
Photography by	Hal Mohr, A.S.C.
Art Direction	Allen Saalburg and Stanley Fleischer
Film Editor	George Amy
Special Photographic Effects	Fred Jackman, A.S.C.
Vitaphone Orchestra conducted by	Leo F. Forbstein
Assistant Director	George Randol

Released: May 1936
Running time: 93 minutes

Cast

De Lawd	Rex Ingram
Gabriel	Oscar Polk
Noah	Eddie Anderson
Moses	Frank Wilson
Mr. Deshee	George Reed
Archangel	Abraham Gleaves
Adam	Rex Ingram
Eve	Myrtle Anderson
Cain	Al Stokes
Zeba	Edna M. Harris
Cain the Sixth	James Fuller
High Priest	George Randol
Noah's Wife	Ida Forsyne
Shem	Ray Martin
Flatfoot	Charles Andrew
Ham	Dudley Dickerson
Japheth	Jimmy Burress
Abraham	William Cumby
Isaac	George Reed
Jacob	Ivory Williams
Aaron	David Bethea
Pharaoh	Ernest Whitman
Head Magician	William Cumby
Joshua	Reginald Fenderson
Master of Ceremonies	Slim Thompson
King of Babylon	William Cumby
Prophet	Clinton Rosamond
Hezdrel	Rex Ingram

Inventory

The following materials from the Warner library of the Wisconsin Center for Film and Theater Research were used by Cripps in preparing *The Green Pastures* for the Wisconsin/Warner Bros. Screenplay Series:

Marc Connelly, *The Green Pastures* (New York: Farrar & Rinehart, 1919), 173 pages.
Temporary, October 23, 1935, 165 pages.
Final, December 31, 1935, with changed pages to March 2, 1936, 160 pages.

DESIGNED BY GARY GORE
COMPOSED BY GRAPHIC COMPOSITION, INC.
ATHENS, GEORGIA
MANUFACTURED BY INTER-COLLEGIATE PRESS, INC.
SHAWNEE MISSION, KANSAS
TEXT AND DISPLAY LINES ARE SET IN PALATINO

Library of Congress Cataloging in Publication Data
Connelly, Marcus Cook, 1890–
The green pastures.
(Wisconsin/Warner Bros. screenplay series)
1. Green pastures. [Motion picture]
I. Cripps, Thomas. II. Green pastures. [Motion picture]
III. Series.
PN1997.G693   791.43'7   79–3959
ISBN 0–299–07920–1
ISBN 0–299–07924–4 pbk.

The Wisconsin/Warner Bros. Screenplay Series, a product of the Warner Brothers Film Library, will enable film scholars, students, researchers, and aficionados to gain insights into individual American films in ways never before possible.

The Warner library was acquired in 1957 by the United Artists Corporation, which in turn donated it to the Wisconsin Center for Film and Theater Research in 1969. The massive library, housed in the State Historical Society of Wisconsin, contains eight hundred sound feature films, fifteen hundred short subjects, and nineteen thousand still negatives, as well as the legal files, press books, and screenplays of virtually every Warner film produced from 1930 until 1950. This rich treasure trove has made the University of Wisconsin one of the major centers for film research, attracting scholars from around the world. This series of published screenplays represents a creative use of the Warner library, both a boon to scholars and a tribute to United Artists.

Most published film scripts are literal transcriptions of finished films. The Wisconsin/Warner screenplays are primary source documents—the final shooting versions including revisions made during production. As such, they will explicate the art of screenwriting as film transcriptions cannot. They will help the user to understand the arts of directing and acting, as well as the other arts involved in the film-making process, in comparing these screenplays with the final films. (Films of the Warner library are available at modest rates from the United Artists nontheatrical rental library, United Artists/16 mm.)

From the eight hundred feature films in the library, the general editor and the editorial committee of the series have chosen those that have received critical recognition for their excellence of directing, screenwriting, and acting, films that are distinctive examples of their genre, those that have particular historical relevance, and some that are adaptations of well-known novels and plays. The researcher, instructor, or student can, in the judicious selection of individual volumes for close examination, gain a heightened appreciation and broad understanding of the American film and its historical role during this critical period.

child.) You want me to come down dere *ve'y* much? You know I said I wouldn't come down. (He looks about; loudly.) Why don' he answer me a little? (Then with a completely bogus dignity, having been thoroughly routed.) Listen! I'll tell you what I'll do. I ain' gonter promise you nothin', an I ain't gonter do nothin' to help you. I'm jes' feelin' a little low, an' I'm only comin' down to make myself feel a little better, dat's all.

He turns and walks out the door, CAMERA PANNING WITH HIM.

463.   MED. SHOT SOLDIERS
picking up wounded.

464.   CLOSE SHOT HEZDREL
The firelight is flickering over his face.

HEZDREL (musingly):
So dey gonter take de temple in de mo'nin'. (He glances up off scene at the temple.) We'll be waitin' for 'em. Jes' remember, boys, when dey kill us we leap out of our skins, right into de lap of God.

A light which does not illuminate the background, but glows about Hezdrel's face, is apparent. The campfire light is no longer noticeable. Hezdrel senses something strange and looks about him. He sees God standing nearby.

465.   CLOSE SHOT HEZDREL AND GOD

GOD:
Hello, Hezdrel—Adam.

HEZDREL:
Who is you?

GOD:
I's an ol' preacher from back in de hills. I jes' got yere. Yo' boys is fightin' bravely, ain't you?

HEZDREL:

We may be killed, but we ain't skeered.

God shows he's pleased.

GOD:

Why is you so brave?

HEZDREL:

Caize, we got faith.

GOD:

Faith? In who?

HEZDREL:

In our dear Lawd God.

GOD:

But didn't he desert you?

HEZDREL:

Not de God we trust in.

GOD:

Who's he?

HEZDREL:

De God of mercy.

GOD (terrified):

But ain't dey only one God?

HEZDREL:

I don't know. But ol' preacher Hosea say not to be skeered of God. Caize he ain't a God of wrath and vengeance no more.

GOD:

Where'd Hosea ever hear about mercy?

HEZDREL:

I guess he found it the same way I found it, the only way anyone can find it.

GOD:
> How's dat?

HEZDREL:
> Through sufferin'.

GOD (proudly):
> You *has* got faith. Even if dey do lick you tomorrow,
> I'll bet de Lawd will be waitin' fo' you.[47]

HEZDREL:
> I know he will.

GOD:
> Thank you, Hezdrel.

HEZDREL:
> Fo' what?

GOD:
> Fo' teachin' me somethin'. I guess, I've been so far
> away, I was behind the times.

God exits. The light fades on Hezdrel. He is again seen
by the illumination of the campfire. There is a trumpet
call. The first soldier enters the scene.

466.   MED. SHOT   HEZDREL AND FIRST SOLDIER

FIRST SOLDIER:
> De cock's jes' crowed, Hezdrel. Dey started fightin'
> ag'in.

The sound of rifle fire and cannon comes over the following speeches.

HEZDREL:
> We's ready. Come on, boys!

467.   MED. SHOT   MEN GATHERING AROUND HEZDREL

HEZDREL:
> Dis is de day dey say dey'll git us. Le's fight till de
> las' man goes. What d'you say?

There are cheers and cries of "Le's go, Hezdrel! "

HEZDREL:
Give 'em ev'thing, boys!

As Hezdrel leads the men, the CAMERA TRUCKS BEFORE THEM. The choir starts to sing "March On."

468. MED. TRUCKING SHOT   HEZDREL AND SOLDIERS
their eyes straight ahead, their faces grimly set, as they march on. The song modulates through the following DISSOLVE to a slow tempo of "Rise, Shine, Give God de Glory."[48]

DISSOLVE TO:

469. FULL SHOT   THE FISH FRY IN HEAVEN
The singing of the choir comes over the SHOT. The illumination is several tones darker than that of the first fish fry scene. The choir is marching more slowly, and the heavenly picnickers are standing in quiet groups about the scene, watching God, who is sitting in an armchair in the center, facing the CAMERA. Gabriel is at his side. The CAMERA MOVES UP TO A

470. CLOSE SHOT   GOD AND GABRIEL

GABRIEL:
You look a little pensive, Lawd. (God nods his head and sighs; he is deep in his thoughts.) Want a seegar, Lawd?

GOD (not looking at Gabriel):
No thanks, Gabriel.

GABRIEL (tenderly):
You look awful pensive, Lawd. You been sittin' yere, lookin' dis way an awful long time. Is it somethin' serious, Lawd?

GOD:
Ve'y serious, Gabriel.